Hyde Park Houses

Hyde Park Houses

AN INFORMAL HISTORY, 1856–1910

Jean F. Block

Photographs by Samuel W. Block, Jr.

The University of Chicago Press, Chicago & London

JEAN F. BLOCK, a native of Hyde Park, has
been president of Midway Editorial Research in
Chicago since 1963.

The University of Chicago Press, Chicago 60637
The University of Chicago Press, Ltd., London

Library of Congress Cataloging in Publication Data

Block, Jean F
    Hyde Park houses.

    Bibliography: p.
    Includes index.
        1. Chicago. Hyde Park.   2. Chicago—Dwellings.
    3. Architecture—Illinois—Chicago.   4. Historic
    buildings—Illinois—Chicago.   I. Block, Samuel W.
    II. Title.
    F548.68.H9B57   977.3'11'04   78-3174
    ISBN 0-226-06000-4

Contents

Illustrations

FIGURES

PLATES

Foreword

The name "Hyde Park" derives from London's 363-acre manor of Hyde. Once a part of the old Westminster Abbey property, the manor became a deer preserve during the reign of Henry VIII, the scene of exciting races at the time of the Stuarts, and the setting of an artificial lake, the Serpentine, during the monarchy of George II. More recently, tourists know it as the site of Rotten Row, with its elegant and aristocratic equestrians, and of Marble Arch and the Speakers' Corner, where generations of soapbox orators have matched wits.

Because this large open space was already famous at the time of the American Revolution, it is hardly surprising that the name was popular in the New World. Hyde Parks were established in Massachusetts, New York, Vermont, Pennsylvania, Illinois, Utah, and Ontario, Canada; that on the east bank of the Hudson River in New York State was designated a National Historic Site in 1944 as the birthplace and home of President Franklin D. Roosevelt.

Although the Hyde Park which is the subject of this volume is an Illinois Historic District and has been nominated for the national designation, it has not yet produced an American president. Indeed, it does not even appear on Illinois maps, having been legally swallowed up when Chicago annexed 130 square miles and a quarter of a million people in the great consolidation of June 29, 1889. Prior to that time, the "Township" of Hyde Park included the entire 48-square-mile area bounded by 35th Street on the north, 138th Street on the south, State Street on the west, and Lake Michigan on the east. Sparsely and irregularly settled, but swelling rapidly from sixteen thousand people in 1880 to eighty-five thousand in 1889, it was not really a town at all, but a collection of twenty-three distinct and disparate communities, including Pullman, Woodlawn, South Chicago, and Grand Crossing.

The "neighborhood" of Hyde Park has always been much smaller than the old "township," and today it includes only those blocks between 47th Street, 59th Street, Cottage Grove Avenue, and the lake. Neither this land area (less than three square miles) nor this population (about seventy thousand at its maximum before urban renewal) is impressive when matched viii

against the thousands of square miles and millions of persons in the Chicago area. But Hyde Park enjoys a very special history and importance. Since 1891 it has been the home of the University of Chicago, an institution of international distinction and influence that has produced and attracted a disproportionate number of writers, scientists, and artists. In 1893, Hyde Park was host to the ten million persons who passed through the gates of the World's Columbian Exposition, the most elaborate and extravagant of all nineteenth-century fairs. In 1942, under the south stands of the university's Stagg Field, the atomic age was born when scientists, working secretly on the Manhattan Project, initiated man's first self-sustaining nuclear reaction. And, finally, in the 1950s, Hyde Park attracted national attention for its pioneering efforts with racial integration and community redevelopment.

From the perspective of urban or architectural history, however, Hyde Park is also important for its role in the history of suburbanization and of residential building. Between 1830, when the mouth of the Chicago River was a mud flat with virtually no year-round inhabitants, and 1910, when the Windy City's population exceeded 1,500,000, Chicago was the fastest-growing major city on earth. It became the home of enormous retailing, manufacturing, and transportation companies that created great fortunes for its leading families. But the very scale and bustle of its emporiums and industries made the city progressively less attractive to affluent residents, who began to associate inner-city neighborhoods with vice, tenements, immigrants, and exhorbitant real estate prices. Increasingly after the Civil War, they began to seek the newer residential sections on the edges of the city. As early as 1873, Everett Chamberlin counted more than one hundred suburbs spreading north and south along the lake and westward toward the prairies. Indeed, it was his assertion that "Chicago, for its size, is more given to suburbs than any other city in the world. In fact, it is doubtful if any city, of any size, can boast of a equal number of suburban appendages."

At mid-century, the quiet village of Hyde Park lay directly in the path of Chicago's southern expansion. In 1856, the Illinois Central Railroad opened its first commuter station at 53d Street and Lake Park Avenue; in 1868, the Chicago and Calumet Railroad inaugurated a second line to the city. By 1873, a dozen trains daily connected Hyde Park with the central business district for a fare of ten cents. By the turn of the century, with the electrification of the streetcar lines and the extension of the elevated system to 63d Street, Hyde Park, like dozens of other once bucolic and isolated villages, had become an integral part of a great metropolis.

As one of the oldest, best-known, and most fashionable of Chicago's suburbs, Hyde Park offered quiet, tree-lined streets, excellent school and church accommodations, and a pronounced upper-middle-class ambiance. Not surprisingly, it attracted the chief executives of many of the Midwest's most important firms—Julius Rosenwald of Sears, Roebuck, R. R. Donnelley of the printing firm bearing his name, Joseph Schaffner of Hart, Schaffner and Marx, W. S. Reed of Chicago and Southern Traction, W. F. Burrows of Libby, McNeill and Libby, Gustavus F. Swift of Swift Packing, to name but a few. Unlike many of the structures built for the barons of New York and Boston, the great mansions of these Chicago millionaires were built on ample lots surrounded by manicured lawns and shrubs. The architectural quality of these opulent dwellings was mixed; some, like Frank Lloyd Wright's Robie House at 58th and Woodlawn, are among the most significant residences in America. Others, such as Martin Ryerson's gray stone Romanesque dwelling, are interesting more for what they reveal about the gargantuan scale of life in the age of conspicuous consumption.

Hyde Park Houses, 1856–1910: An Informal History provides us with the first comprehensive look at these monuments to an earlier time. But the real achievement of Jean F. Block does not lie in her consideration of structures important either for their design or their bulk. Rather, she has investigated an entire neighborhood, not excluding the modest dwellings of the lower middle class. On Blackstone Avenue, for example, as many as six houses were crowded onto a one-hundred-foot lot, an illustration of the fact that the enormous expansion of Hyde Park between 1860 and 1910 created opportunities for young architects who were willing to design homes for a variety of income groups. Unlike Lake Forest or Winnetka, Hyde Park never acquired a reputation as an exclusive preserve of the very rich. Instead, as the author emphasizes, it was really three separate areas: Kenwood, Hyde Park Center, and South Park. If the residents of the area between Harper and Woodlawn, 53d and 55th Streets, could not hope to emulate aristocratic Kenwood, they nevertheless could and did fulfill their dream of a single-family house on a private lot.

Although Jean Block places the architectural history of the neighborhood within the larger framework of the community's economic and cultural life, she has not pretended to write a complete history of Hyde Park. Instead, she focuses on a single field (architecture), a single type of structure (residences), and a single time period (1856–1910). Urban historians will recognize that the author uses neither the methodology nor the jargon of the academic profession. This lack of scholarly pretension and expertise, however, should not obscure the fact that the sources and objectives of this book tie in very nicely with what is sometimes called "the new urban history." Mrs. Block has analyzed the construction dates, architects, and ownership of more than nine hundred homes, and she has provided biographical sketches of the more than forty architects who designed three or more dwellings in Hyde Park, an effort that required extensive work with such relatively "new" urban history sources as city permits, county building records, specialized construction and architectural periodicals, city directories, local newspapers, and personal interviews. More than seventy-five of the homes have been photographed for this volume; if the reader examines these delightful pictures and correlates them with the text, he will learn a great deal about both architecture and history. Information about houses which have not been included in the photographs may be found in an appendix organized by street.

Hyde Park Houses should be seen as part of a renewed interest in the built environment that has been gathering strength since the brownstoning movement began in Brooklyn, Philadelphia, Boston, and Washington in the late 1940s. Although newer, FHA-financed, tract homes in the suburbs offered curvilinear streets, large garages and closets, modern kitchens and bathrooms, and spacious lawns, few indeed could match the high ceilings or wide-planked floors, elaborate molding or carved fireplaces, Queen Anne facades or solid doors that were common in older dwellings. The renovation and restoration of such houses have proceeded with incredible rapidity in the last fifteen years, but even those who have little interest in historic preservation have come to realize that the shortage of energy may have profound implications for urban life in the decades to come. For example, the National League of Cities recently reported that redevelopment of older neighborhoods, when it is compared with typical, low-density suburban sprawl, results in 44 percent less capital costs, 43 percent less land costs and energy consumption, 50 percent less auto emissions, and 35 percent less water consumption.

Neighborhood history is as yet an undeveloped field, as is the study of "average" or "typical" houses. Happily, a new trend seems to be developing. The two most distinguished books in this field are Sam Bass Warner's *Streetcar Suburbs: The Process of Growth in Boston, 1870–1900* (Cambridge: Harvard University Press, 1962); and Bainbridge Bunting, *Houses of Boston's Back Bay: An Architectural History, 1840–1917* (Cambridge: Harvard University Press, 1967), but other historians have recently begun to add to the list. *Hyde Park Houses* reminds us that the history of cities is really the history of the growth and transition of constantly evolving neighborhoods. Jean Block's book can be read with pleasure and with profit by those who have lived in, worked in, or visited any neighborhood that is rich with associations of people who played important roles in American life and letters, as well as by those whose primary interests are the larger processes epitomized by the wood, brick, and stone of Hyde Park.

KENNETH T. JACKSON

Columbia University

Preface

This book is intended to show how, in the period between 1856 and 1910, a prairie settlement metamorphosed into a heavily populated and thriving urban neighborhood. The story of this growth, to which geographical, economic, political, social, and intellectual forces all contributed, can still be read in the streetscapes of the neighborhood and in the architecture of its houses.

The neighborhood is Hyde Park–Kenwood, in Chicago, approximately eight miles south of the center of the city. The area covered extends from 47th Street to 59th Street, and from Cottage Grove Avenue to Lake Michigan. In one sense Hyde Park–Kenwood is an artifact carved out of a larger inner-city neighborhood by an urban renewal program of the 1950s and 1960s. Before that time the north and south boundaries were less firmly fixed.

Hyde Park–Kenwood is not an ancestor-worshiping community. When I began to look into its past, I found few letters, diaries, or books annotating or commemorating it. Its first public buildings—the town hall, the churches, the public school, the original Illinois Central stations—have long since disappeared. But we do have the houses. They are the material remains of the early culture of the first fifty years. They indicate how and why the community grew. They are the tale and signature of the past, unwittingly bequeathed by their owners and builders. To walk the streets is to see displayed the story of midwestern people and their homes, from workingmen's cottages to mansions, from pattern-book villas to houses designed by some of Chicago's best architects, among them Holabird and Roche, Treat and Foltz, Frost and Granger, Flanders and Zimmerman, Handy and Cady, Alfred Alschuler, Howard Van Doren Shaw, Dwight Perkins, Pond and Pond, George Maher, Hugh Garden, Horatio Wilson, Benjamin Marshall, and Frank Lloyd Wright.

There are so many architects and so many significant buildings that it is impossible to discuss them all within the context of the community's development. Appendix A lists all architects who built three or more dwellings in the area and supplies biographical material on them. Appendix B is a checklist of existing dwellings built before 1910 and should help readers who want to locate the work of less prolific builders. The checklist also gives the name and occupation of the first owner of each building when this information is available.

Like most nineteenth-century community histories, as well as many of those compiled for the U.S. Bicentennial celebration, this one springs from a lifelong experience with the neighborhood. I grew up in Hyde Park–Kenwood and my husband and I returned there to raise our family after World War II. I have always been fascinated by its history and beguiled by its domestic architecture. As a place to live it offers a wide variety of experiences, visual, intellectual, and social. Tracing the course of its development and searching out and identifying the houses, their owners, and the architects have illuminated many of the reasons for this richness and diversity.

I should like to express my appreciation to the Illinois Arts Council for a grant that made the project possible. I am also deeply grateful to Michael Young, who has patiently and cheerfully performed many dull tasks, and to Samuel W. Block, Jr., whose fine photographs enliven the text. The maps were prepared by Christopher Müller-Wille. Neil Harris, Joseph Connors, and Arthur Mann have offered encouragement and valuable suggestions. The comments of Zane Miller, Kenneth T. Jackson, and Roy Forrey have aided me in strengthening the text. Neal J. Ney, Larry Viskochil, and Julia Westerberg, all of the Chicago Historical Society, Annette Fern, of the Burnham Library of the Art Institute of Chicago, Mark Friedberger of the Newberry Library and Catharine Karasek of the R. R. Donnelley Lakeside Press have been of great assistance. Albert Tannler, archivist in the University of Chicago Library's Department of Special Collections, has been unflagging in his interest and aid. The Chicago Title Insurance Company graciously supplied needed information. The Illinois Central Gulf Railroad through Robert W. O'Brien generously offered photographs. Paul Adrien Cornell and John E. Cornell, Jr., gave their fullest cooperation in assembling the material on their illustrious ancestor. Friends and neighbors too numerous to mention have contributed eagerly. I want to thank especially Joan Hall, Albert and Thelma Dahlberg, Leon and Marian Despres, Gavin Williamson, George Fred Keck, Florence Miller, Robert McDougal, Jane Stevens, Margrette Dornbusch, Ruth Billingsley, Noble Lee, Dorothy Hendricks, Helene Billings, Father Thomas J. Fitzgerald, Robert Wagner, Malcolm Collier, Muriel Beadle, Carroll Russell, and Irma Strauss. Ruth Grodzins has made valuable editorial suggestions, and Eleanor Pettigrew has been a forbearing typist.

J. F. B.

The Perfect Suburb 1856–71

Fig. 1

Paul Cornell: Practical Dreamer

In 1852, when Paul Cornell commissioned a topographical survey of land south of Chicago, that great octopus of a city was growing at an astonishing rate. Situated at the junction of Lake Michigan with the inland waterways and five railroad lines, Chicago drew in and sent out food, raw materials, and manufactured goods. It was both a shipping center and a manufacturing center, processing grain into flour, cattle into meat, timber into lumber, and metal into farm implements. With its unrivaled communications and access to raw materials, it presented irresistible challenges to eager and ambitious businessmen. Muddy in winter, dusty in summer, odorous with wastes, however, it was an unpleasant place in which to live, and the movement out from the center, toward green and quiet sanctuaries, had already started at mid-century.

Thirty-year-old Paul Cornell was aware of this trend; he knew, too, from what he had observed in the East, that one of the marvels of the steam railway was that it could transport people as well as goods. He sensed that the period of isolation for people who lived outside the cities was almost over: the railroad would bring them into physical contact; the newly invented telegraph would keep them in touch with events throughout the country.

He was also a capitalist. In those days the word did not carry the pejorative connotation with which Marx and his followers later endowed it. Capitalism simply meant using your money to make more money, and the belief in the real estate world was that if you didn't do that, you were short-sighted or slow-witted or both. Indeed, the prevailing notion was that what was good for business was good for people in general.

In 1853, Cornell purchased his three hundred acres between 51st and 55th streets, deeding sixty to the Illinois Central Railroad in exchange for the promise of a passenger station.[1] It is reasonable to assume that he was thinking of the inevitable rise in land values as the city continued to grow.

Fig. 1. Paul Cornell, from a daguerreotype, undated.
(Courtesy of the Chicago Historical Society)

The land that he bought had been Indian domain until the treaty that ended the Black Hawk War in 1832. Charles Butler described it in a letter telling of his trip from New York to Chicago in 1833. Filled with the spirit of adventure, he had come to see the newly opened territory: "I approached Chicago in the afternoon of a beautiful day, the 2nd of August [1833]; the sun setting in a cloudless sky. On my left lay the prairie, bounded only by the distant horizon like a vast expanse of ocean; on my right, in the summer stillness, lay Lake Michigan. I had never seen anything more beautiful or captivating in nature. There was an entire absence of animal life, nothing visible in the way of human habitation or to indicate the presence of man, and yet it was a scene full of life; for there spread out before me in every direction, as far as the eye could reach, were the germs of life in earth, air, and water."[2]

The road Butler took was the old military and stagecoach road which ran round the bottom of the lake from Detroit to Chicago. He was fortunate to have been traveling in August, rather than winter or spring, when the road was often so muddy it could be traversed only on foot. Inland from the sandy shore lay stretches of marsh threaded with meandering streams. Beyond to the west and ahead to the north could be seen oak groves. The long grass was alight with prairie flowers.

Although the land south of the city was offered for settlement by the United States government, and even put up for auction in New York City in 1835, there seem to have been few takers. Obadiah Hooper homesteaded eighty acres bounded by the present 55th and 59th streets, and Woodlawn and Dorchester avenues, only to disappear, never heard of again. This property was subject to constant litigation and sold repeatedly for payment of back taxes at the north door of the courthouse.[3] In 1847 William Egan, a brilliant physician, pioneer Chicagoan, and expansive speculator in real estate, purchased a large irregular tract between what are now 47th and 55th streets, Cottage Grove and Woodlawn, planning to reproduce an Irish country estate. He hired Irish gardeners to plant trees and construct ornamental mounds on the flat grasslands and laid a winding country road through the estate. He was apparently overextended and underfinanced, however, because his beautiful scheme never materialized.[4] After his death in 1860 the land was acquired by George C. Smith, a Chicago banker, and the Drexel family of Philadelphia; nevertheless, it retained the name Egandale for many years.

Cornell was not alone in his dreams of a suburb. Evanston was in the making, and Cornell's wife was a sister-in-law of John Evans for whom that town was named; another sister was married to Orrington Lunt, one of the founders of Northwestern University; still a third was the wife of George Kimbark, who later became an officer and director of the Riverside Improvement Company, which developed Chicago's most ambitious and successful planned suburb.[5]

Cornell envisioned a middle- and upper-class suburb that would serve both as a retreat for Chicago's business and professional men and their families and as a summer resort. His grand scheme included seven key elements: transportation, a neat plan, a clean industry-free environment, an institution that would employ residents and provide a stable population, a hotel, a church, and parks.

The railroad connection with nearby Chicago was Cornell's basic ingredient. The Illinois Central opened Chicago's first suburban passenger station at 53d and Lake Park in 1856.

Cornell's second requirement was that Hyde Park resemble a neat New England or New York village. The flat prairie land that had never been broken up into farms and was nowhere heavily forested lent itself readily to the geometry of a grid street pattern. The settlement clustered around the station, and to this configuration Cornell added a small park on the lakefront, at first called the Common.

The community was to be solely residential, with only those businesses needed to provide amenities and necessities for the inhabitants. Cornell's investments in land for industrial purposes were to the south and west; his watch factory was built at Grand Crossing. Hyde Park was to be spared the fumes, noises, and refuse of developing industry.

Cornell wanted a lakeside institution, like Evanston's Northwestern University, to anchor the community, and he set aside some of his shoreland to establish a Presbyterian theological seminary. This plan was frustrated, however, by the presbytery's decision to build the seminary on the North Side.

But he was highly successful in his plan to build a hotel. Hyde Park House, at 53d and the lake, opened in 1857, the same year that Cornell brought his family to live in Hyde Park. It was an elegant resort hotel, gaslit, prettily landscaped, hospitably verandahed. It was the center of the community's social life and the scene of many summer festivities. Because it could be reached easily from downtown Chicago by boat, carriage, or train, it became a favorite vacation spot for city families. Mothers and children could enjoy the wholesome country air and the pleasures of the lake while fathers commuted to work. And many famous people came to visit, to take tea or dinner, or to make more prolonged stays. Albert Edward, prince of Wales, was taken to Hyde Park House when he visited Chicago in 1860, and Mrs. Lincoln and her sons retreated there after the president's assassination.[6]

The spiritual as well as the material and social needs of the community had to be met, and so Paul Cornell gave the people of Hyde Park a little church, also at 53d Street, which was shared by the Presbyterian and Episcopal congregations until each could put up its own building.

Unlike village churches in the East, however, this church had no graveyard. In the same year, 1853, that Cornell bought his 300 acres, a group of Chicagoans, convinced of the future growth of the city, purchased 167 acres south of 67th Street and incorporated Oak Woods Cemetery, making plans for a garden cemetery with naturalized landscaping and four artificial lakes. J. Y. Scammon was president, Paul Cornell, secretary.[7]

Finally, Cornell dreamed of an ambitious scheme for a park system that would serve both the local residents and the city of Chicago, to which the parks would be connected by landscaped boulevards.

Investors and Settlers

Many of the first purchasers and first residents were Cornell's relatives and friends. His uncle, Hassan A. Hopkins, bought the Obadiah Hooper land in 1859, and this became Hopkins' Addition to Hyde Park. His brother-in-law, George Kimbark, acquired a piece of land between 51st and 55th streets, Dorchester and Woodlawn, which became Kimbark's Addition to Hyde Park. Later Cornell bought both these tracts. Men who were at various times Cornell's law partners, John Jameson, Charles B. Waite, Homer N. Hibbard, Junius Mulvey, and William T. Barron were early settlers. Although these first investors combined their real

5

Fig. 2. Paul Cornell's house at what is now 51st and Harper. (Courtesy of the Chicago Historical Society)

Fig. 3. Hyde Park House, 1859. The hotel burned in 1879. (Courtesy of the Chicago Historical Society)

estate dealings with other business or professional work, there were also those who made real estate a full-time activity, such as the Bogues, who moved to Hyde Park in 1858.

As the little community was gathering in Hyde Park, a few people were also moving into Kenwood. In 1856 Jonathan Kennicott built a small frame house for his family at Dorchester and 48th Street. He was a dentist who had his office in the city but indulged his passion for horticulture by living in the country. The name Kenwood was derived from Kennicott's ancestral home in Scotland, and when the Illinois Central in 1859 provided a passenger station at 47th Street, it was called Kenwood Station.[8] One wonders if different attitudes toward the new community are betrayed by the names chosen by Cornell and Kennicott. According to Cornell's family, Hyde Park was named for Hyde Park, London, an urban area of pleasure grounds and boulevards, whereas Kenwood was apparently named for a rural retreat.

Figs. 4, 5

At this time, too, Chicagoans J. H. Lyman, Edwin C. Larned, and John Woodbridge purchased and subdivided land from 47th to 49th streets, Dorchester to Woodlawn, and another large tract from 47th to 51st, Woodlawn to Ellis. This was purely investment property. None of these men ever lived in Kenwood. Lyman and Larned, like others who made land purchases, were friends of Cornell. By April 1859 Lyman was advertising for sale two two-story houses, each with an acre of land.[9] Other early settlers in Kenwood were William Waters and John Remmer, employees of the Illinois Central, and Pennoyer Sherman, a downtown lawyer.

A third railroad station was opened at 57th Street, initially known as Woodville, because that was where the train refueled. Later it was called South Park. An early resident there was Samuel Fassett, a pioneer Chicago photographer. William Hoyt, a real estate broker, and Claudius B. Nelson, who combined the hardware business with real estate development, came somewhat later.[10]

A Separate Township

Hyde Park was originally in the same township as the village of Lake, which lay west of State Street. Very early it became obvious that the settlements along the Illinois Central tracks had more in common with each other than they did with those to the west. The railroad not only provided an essential link with the city but the daily trips to and from Chicago developed in its riders a sense of community: common interests were discussed, plans made, friendships cultivated. There was no public transportation from Hyde Park to the town meetings on State Street, nor did the Hyde Parkers feel that there were many shared concerns. Homer N. Hibbard was commissioned to go to Springfield and to request a special act of incorporation for Hyde Park. He succeeded, and the town was incorporated in 1861. It was bounded by

ILLINOIS CENTRAL RAILROAD.

Hyde Park and Oak Woods Train,

TIME TABLE.

TO TAKE EFFECT, MAY 2d, 1869.

GOING SOUTH.					Daily, except Sundays	GOING NORTH.				
P. M.	P. M.	P. M.	P. M.	A. M.	*Leave. | Arrive.*	A. M.	A. M.	P. M.	P. M.	P. M.
6.10	5.15	3.00	12.10	6 20	..Central Depot..	7.45	9 45	1.40	5 15	7.35
6.18	....	3.08	12.18	6 28	....12th Street....	7.37	....	1.32	5.07	7.27
6.20	4 20	3.10	12.20	6 30	..... Weldon	7.35	9.05	1.30	5.05	7.25
6.21	....	3.11	12.21	6.31	....18th Street....	7.33	....	1.27	5.00	7.23
6.23	4.22	3.13	12.22	6 32	....22d Street....	7.31	9.02	1.25	4.58	7.22
6.26	....	3.15	12.25	6.35	....Car Works....	7.30		1.24	4.56	7.20
6.32	....	3.23	12.30	6.40	.....Fairview.....	7.25	....	1.20	4.52	7.15
6.34	4.30	3.25	12.32	6.42	....Oakland	7.23	8.47	1.18	4.50	7.12
6.37	.	3.28	12.34	6.44	..Reform School .	7.20	....	1.15	4.49	7.10
6.40	4.35	3.34	12.36	6.46	.....Kenwood.....	7.17	8.44	1.12	4.47	7.08
6.44	4.39	3.35	12.40	6.50	....Hyde Park....	7.15	8.42	1.08	4.44	7.05
6.46	....	3.37	12.42	6.52	....Woodville ...	7.13	....	1.03	4.42	7.03
6.50	4.43	3.40	12.45	6.55	....Wood Lawn.	7.10	8.38	1.00	4.35	7.00
6.52	....	3.45	12.50	7.00	....Oak Woods....	7.05	....	12.55	4.32	6.58
P. M.	P. M.	P. M.	P. M.	A. M.	*Arrive. | Leave.*	A. M.	A. M.	P. M.	P. M.	P. M.

M. HUGHITT. Gen'l Superintendent.

OVER.

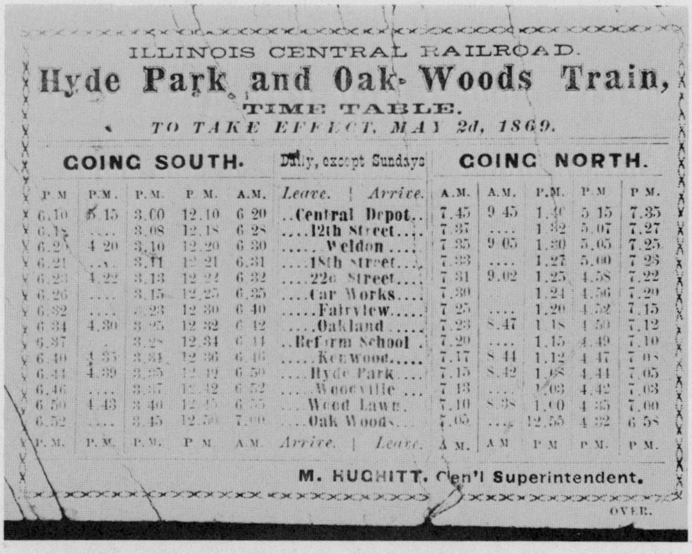

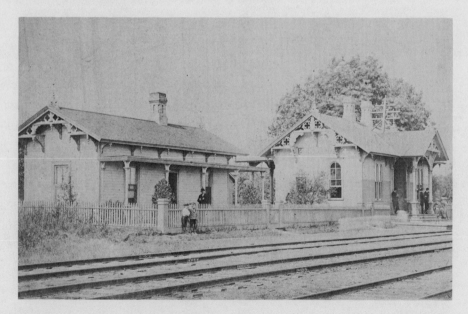

Fig. 4. Illinois Central timetable, 1869. Woodville was the 57th Street station, so called because that was where the train refueled. The suburban train provided convenient transportation to Oak Woods Cemetery. (Courtesy of the Illinois Central Gulf Railroad)

Fig. 5. The Kenwood Station on the Illinois Central, about 1882. (Courtesy of the Chicago Historical Society)

8

Fig. 6. Kenwood School, 1880. Saint Paul's Episcopal
Church can be seen to the right. (Courtesy of the Chicago
Historical Society)

39th Street on the north, what is now 138th Street on the south, State Street on the west, and
Lake Michigan and the Indiana border on the east. Within the north end of the larger political
entity known as Hyde Park Township were the three smaller communities, Kenwood,
Hyde Park Center, and South Park. Thirty years later South Park became the site of the
University of Chicago.

Hyde Park's first town meeting was held on April 2, 1861, in the 53d Street Illinois
Central station; Paul Cornell was elected supervisor. Other officers were town clerk, collector,
two highway commissioners, two justices of the peace, two constables, and a pound master.[11]

Adding Services

The stage was set. It remained but to drop into place the sustaining services. Cornell's uncle,
Hassan A. Hopkins, who was also town clerk, opened a grocery store. George C. Waite,
surveyor, real estate investor, and collector for the township, established a postoffice and
became postmaster. Cornell, Hibbard, and Jameson arranged for a public school.[12] In 1867 an

amendment in the town charter provided for a board of trustees composed of the supervisor, collector, assessor, and two commissioners of highways. In 1868 Chauncey M. Cady, the music publisher, was made president of the trustees, an office he held for four years. The Presbyterians, the Episcopalians, and the Roman Catholics built their churches. And, in 1869, the north-south commuter line was augmented by the Chicago and Calumet's steam dummy that moved across 55th Street to Cottage Grove and thence downtown.[13] ("Dummy" referred to the housing built around the engine so that it would not frighten horses.)

The town officials applied themselves to the problems of building streets, sidewalks, sewers, and drains. Plans were made for improving Hyde Park Avenue (now Lake Park) by laying a broad bed of Joliet gravel from the city limits to 57th Street. Work proceeded on Stony Island Avenue, which would connect what is now the southwest corner of Jackson Park with Lake Calumet. The road was built by first laying a platform of boards on the mud and water, then adding a thick layer of swamp grass or reeds, and lastly dumping gravel on the foundation until it began to sink. As C. M. Cady remarked, "This will insure a solid, durable roadbed upon a slough that has probably never before been crossed safely, except by birds and muskrats."[14]

The Second Wave of Newcomers

Chicago became a center of Civil War activity, and after the war business continued to boom, the population increasing yearly. The demand for land outside the city limits was, if anything, even greater than it was when Paul Cornell bought his first acres. Land values rose steadily, as did the demand for housing.

Purchasers and builders fell into two by no means separate and distinct groups: those who wanted homes to live in and those who planned to invest or speculate in land or to build houses for rent or sale.

Many prominent Chicagoans moved into Hyde Park and Kenwood during this period, men who had been successful in the world of law and business, men who had participated in state and national politics. Active, enterprising, shapers of their own world, they knew each other not only through their work but also through their voluntary activities, serving together on the boards of the Chicago Relief and Aid Society, the Chicago Academy of Sciences, the Chicago Historical Society.

Among these men was Jonathan Young Scammon, a pioneer Chicagoan, founder of the first Swedenborgian church, lawyer, banker, conoisseur of art and literature, intimate of Lincoln, who had his summer home at "Fernwood," a wooded stretch on 59th Street between Dorchester and Woodlawn. James P. Root, director of Hyde Park's schools from 1862 to 1864, was also closely associated with Lincoln and in charge of his 1864 campaign. Lyman Trumbull, U.S. Senator during these years, owned a house a little to the north of 47th Street. Norman Judd, an early law associate of Scammon, returned to his Kenwood home between tours of duty as minister to Prussia during the Lincoln administration and while serving in Congress. W. K. Ackerman, local treasurer of the Illinois Central, and later its president, was one of Kenwood's early residents, as was lawyer Charles Hitchcock who presided over the Illinois constitutional convention in 1870. John Dunham, sugar merchant and banker, and B. P. Hutchinson, grain and provisions dealer and speculator, both owned summer estates in the neighborhood. Judge Hollis Van Higgins's house at 50th and Woodlawn was the scene of many parties and benefits.

The Population in 1870

To this galaxy of glittering names could be added those of many other successful Chicago business and professional men. But contrary to what guidebooks of the time might lead one to believe, this was not exclusively a middle- and upper-class community, nor was it made up solely of white Protestants from the eastern states. The 1870 United States census shows that the first group of a dozen or so families in Hyde Park–Kenwood had grown to more than two hundred families—over a thousand people in all. In addition to the seventy-five businessmen and forty-seven professionals, there were seventy-nine skilled workers—carpenters, masons, plumbers, and gardeners; thirty-three common laborers, and more than a hundred domestic servants, both male and female. Except for domestic service, the only woman's occupation listed is "keeping house." The lawyers formed the largest professional group (sixteen); there were also fifteen teachers and five clergymen, but only two doctors. Of the businessmen, twenty-two were engaged in wholesale or manufacturing enterprises, six were financiers, ten were in the real estate business, sixteen identified themselves as managers; the rest operated or were employed in various retail businesses, such as food and clothing stores, in the city.

These business and professional people had come from the eastern states, as had most of the skilled workers. The domestic servants tended to be Scandinavian and Irish, with a scattering of English, Scots, and Germans. Although the foreign-born made up almost half the population of Chicago at this time, in Hyde Park–Kenwood they comprised slightly fewer than one-third of the residents. There were eight blacks, five of whom were domestic servants. Three were children, two brothers and a girl, living in the home of Jonathan Kennicott. The common laborers were chiefly Irish, forming a labor pool for the superintendent of public works, himself an Irishman. They lived in the workingmen's cottages on streets adjacent to Saint Thomas the Apostle Roman Catholic church, at the corner of 55th and Kimbark.

Households were large: two-thirds of them contained five or more persons, including children, relatives, domestic servants, and lodgers. Except for Hyde Park House, which does not appear on the census and apparently was occupied chiefly by transients, the only accommodation for single persons was as boarders in homes. This was true of unmarried teachers and clergymen as well as newcomers from Ireland and Scandinavia, who lodged with countrymen while seeking employment.

All levels of railroad employees were represented: managers, freight agents, engineers, conductors, and laborers in the car works. The importance of the lake in Chicago's transportation system is pointed up by the presence in the community of five ship captains, one seaman, and a ship's carpenter. Retail businesses were confined to a few grocery stores, two meat markets, two florist's shops, a pharmacy, the establishments of an ice dealer and a coal dealer, and two saloons. Notably absent were clothing and drygoods stores, dressmakers, tailors, shoemakers, and cafés and restaurants. The one restaurant proprietor listed probably ran the hotel dining room.

Half of the household heads owned real estate, and over one-third of them valued their holdings at more than $5,000—more, that is, than could be accounted for by a house and lot. Eight residents owned real estate worth more than $100,000. Paul Cornell estimated his holdings at $600,000 and his personal wealth at $300,000. He was said to have had only $1.50 in his pocket when he came to Chicago in 1847, and that was stolen soon after he arrived.

Planning for the South Parks

The high land values may be attributed at least in part to the prospective development of Paul Cornell's park system. Discussions of a possible park system began in 1866 among Paul Cornell, George Kimbark, Chauncey Bowen, George R. Clarke, Obadiah Jackson, Jonathan Y. Scammon and J. Irving Pearce, most of whom owned property in Hyde Park Township. They wrote for information to various cities, both in this country and abroad, studying the parks of great capitals for a way to provide public pleasure grounds which would, as Cornell put it, give lungs to a great city and its future generations. This was a phrase used frequently by nineteenth-century planners and developers. It expressed their distress about the unhealthiness of city life and its remoteness from nature.

As a result of their investigations and discussions, these men were able to submit a bill to the state legislature setting forth provisions for their park development program. There were to be five Chicago commissioners appointed by the governor, bonds not to exceed $1,000,000, and a yearly tax not to exceed $200,000. The park was to be somewhere south of 35th Street and north of 63d Street.

Cornell spent the winter of 1867 in Springfield lobbying for the bill. He was successful, and the bill was submitted to the people of Hyde Park Township for a special vote in the spring election. But, whether through misunderstanding, lack of information, or chicanery, it was defeated by the voters. The following year, however, a new bill was enacted, this time specifying the location of the parks and boulevards; it was passed in the referendum, thus establishing the South Park system, which included what are now Washington Park, Jackson Park, and the Midway Plaisance connecting them.[15]

In 1869, while the park commissioners were still acquiring land, and not without some protests about the prices they were paying for it, Calvert Vaux, of the New York landscaping firm of Olmsted and Vaux, came to Chicago to work on the planned community of Riverside. He conferred with the commissioners and they engaged his firm to draw up surveys, working plans, and specifications for the South Park system. Like New York's Central Park, which had been Olmsted and Vaux's pioneering design, the site was chiefly wasteland. Jackson Park was sandy and marshy. What is now the lagoon in Jackson Park was a natural water hole known as Phillips Creek. Washington Park was treeless prairie.

But Frederick Law Olmsted and Calvert Vaux believed that parks, by providing beauty and pleasure for the people, could also make them better human beings. Closeness to nature would counteract the evils of the industrialized city, heighten their sensitivity to beauty, and make them finer citizens. They drew elaborate plans that included woodland walks, facilities for concerts, theatrical performances, boating, and swimming, as well as an aviary and places where deer, sheep, goats, and cattle could browse. The ambition and scope of their designs was dazzling, and it looked very much as if the parks would materialize.[16] The project was suspended, however, when the South Park Commission offices in the *Tribune* building were destroyed, along with all their plans, contracts, and accounts, in the great Chicago Fire.

The Chicago Fire

The great fire of October 8–10, 1871, consumed the city from Taylor Street to Fullerton Avenue, devastating twenty-two hundred acres and destroying eighteen thousand buildings. Starting at 8:45 Sunday evening, driven by a strong southwest wind, it raged until Tuesday morning, when it burned itself out at the northeast edge of the city. Although the fire did not spread southward, people in Hyde Park–Kenwood could see the flames and the reddened sky.

School was dismissed at ten in the morning, and the children rushed to the lakeshore to watch the fire within the city. Thousands of people were injured, three hundred died, and over ninety thousand lost their homes. The trains offered free transportation to the homeless who wanted to leave the city, and many were quartered in Hyde Park–Kenwood. Return trains bore supplies of food and clothing, blankets, and other necessities, to which many fortunate enough to have been outside the fire boundaries contributed eagerly. Church members were mobilized to offer relief and assistance.

Mrs. Norman Judd wrote to Mrs. Mark Skinner from her Kenwood home in late November: "Those of us who still have houses and clothing are busy caring for sufferers every spare moment . . . . We have been very busy taking care of the families who have come into Hyde Park. Last week we made clothing for a baby a month old, and who had been wrapped in an old blanket & never worn a garment & before the fire the parents were people in good circumstances surrounded by every comfort . . . . We hope every week that we shall find some limit to our work, but the throng who come to the church where we hold our meetings was as large as ever yesterday. We meet on Fridays at the church at Hyde Park and on Tuesdays at Mrs. Higgins' to sew and give out supplies."[17]

Pre-Fire Houses in Hyde Park–Kenwood

Because the fire destroyed most of Chicago's frame houses, those that escaped in outlying areas assume special importance as early examples of *balloon framing,* an innovation in building technique that originated in Chicago in the 1830s. With traditional framing (which continued for many years to be used in building barns), the skeleton of a wooden house consisted of massive eight- to twelve-inch-square corner posts and cross members mortised and tenoned together. When the main structure had been raised and fastened in place, an operation that required the efforts of a number of strong men (as in the traditional "barn raising"), vertical wall members (*studs*) were inserted in the outer framing, where they served mainly as a base to which the siding materials could be fastened. Balloon framing employed very light materials— commonly two-by-fours—which could be handled by one man, in place of massive timbers, and the studding formed an integral, strength-giving part of the frame. Moreover, the balloon frame was put together with common nails rather than intricate mortise-and-tenon joints, which required woodworking skills of a high order to construct.[18]

The advent of balloon framing had to await the arrival of two earlier innovations in building technology—cheap, machine-made nails (which came in the late eighteenth century) and the availability in plenty of small-dimension lumber (which followed the invention of the power-driven circular saw in the second decade of the nineteenth century). One inventive Chicago builder—some say it was Augustine D. Taylor, some, George W. Snow—put these elements together in a new type of light frame that literally revolutionized the art of building in wood. Using the balloon frame, one man of only moderate carpentry skills, preferably with a helper, could erect an entire house.

Use of the balloon frame spread rapidly from Chicago, and from coast to coast houses were soon being erected by this method. Balloon framing also made prefabrication possible, and by 1860 several firms in New York, Boston, and Chicago were prepared to ship precut portions of buildings to any rail terminal in the country. Pieces were numbered and could be joined together with nails or bolts to form houses, schools, or stores. The lumber for these houses was cheap and readily available, arriving on ships from the forests across the lake.[19]

Chicago became a city of wooden houses—and wooden sidewalks as well—which, made dry as tinder by a rainless summer, disappeared in flames in less than two days' time. The fire ordinance that was passed after the catastrophe made building frame houses within the city limits illegal. People continued to build in wood outside the fire limits until the end of the nineteenth century, however, even after annexation: Chicago was so eager to acquire the suburban areas that the fire laws were waived to entice them to join the city. Thus one curious result of the fire was that Hyde Park–Kenwood became, in effect, an architectural museum in which one can observe the development of the frame house.

Although most of the pre-fire houses in this area are gone, enough remain to show us what they were like. At 5630 Kimbark one of the earliest houses, with the rounded windows typical of the Italianate style, is in an excellent state of preservation. It was probably built in the late 1860s, and according to the present owner its barn stood at Woodlawn and 56th. A stream lined with willows is described as having run through what is now the alley between Kimbark and Woodlawn, eventually emptying into Lake Michigan near the foot of 63d Street. A few willows, full of migrating warblers every spring, can still be found on the alley.

Pl. 1

The house at 5607 Dorchester was also built before the fire. The bracketed roof and vestigial cupola, as well as the double door and wide-columned verandah, are typical of the period. At one time the house probably had a wing on the north, to match that on the south.

Pl. 2

South of this house, at 5642 Dorchester, is another pre-1871 house, somewhat altered. Its little barn is the last remaining example of vertical "board-and-batten" siding in Hyde Park. The size of the barn, large enough for a horse and carriage (but not for other farm animals or equipment), suggests that this was, even in the sixties, a suburban house rather than a farm.

Pl. 3

John Drury, in *Old Chicago Houses,* describes both 5704 and 5714 Dorchester. Although he gives 1874 as the date for the Hoyt house at 5704, Hoyt, a real estate broker, is listed in the *Edwards* directory as living in Hyde Park in 1869; thus it seems that this house was built at

Pls. 4, 5

least that early, making it one of the pre-fire houses. Both of these dwellings are capacious, squarely built, and gracious in the popular Italianate style. The verandahs have been cut down, but part of the cupola remains on 5714. When this house was built, it must have commanded a fine view of the lake. Claudius B. Nelson bought it in the late sixties; the property included all of the east side of Kenwood to 58th Street, and all of the west side of Dorchester.

Pl. 6

At 5417 Blackstone is another Italianate bracketed house with the side bay also characteristic of the time. Simpler cottages were beginning to appear in this area. The balloon-framed "Chicago cottage," built for the workingman and his family, became a part of the local scene. Chicago cottages are difficult to date, because they were constructed routinely over a period of at least thirty years, from the early sixties to the middle nineties. Commenting on the supposedly innovative designs for workingmen's houses at the 1893 Columbian Exposition, *Inland Architect* observed that none of them was so livable or practical as the Chicago cottage. Balloon-framed of millwork, embellished with whatever wood trim their owners found attractive and could afford, these houses were also designed to be movable. If a laborer found a better job in another part of the city, he could lift up his house and take it with him.[20] They could be enlarged as well, either by the addition of another floor or by raising the whole house and putting a brick first floor underneath. A number of these cottages survive on Dorchester and

Pl. 7

Blackstone. Many, however, like this one, have been covered with abestos siding.

Modest houses like these were not always built by laborers or for laborers. In 1860 Henry C. Work, composer of such Civil War songs as "Marching through Georgia," "Kingdom Coming," and "Wake Nicodemus," as well as the sentimental temperance song "Father, Dear Father,

Pl. 8

Come Home with Me Now," built the small cottage at the back of 5317 Dorchester with his own hands on land purchased from Paul Cornell. The front part, also typically Chicago cottage style, was added in 1867.

Only two houses remain in Kenwood from this period. At 1357–59 East 48th Street is a double house, built by Jonathan Kennicott in about 1867. Although much altered, it still retains many features of the period: the bracketed roof, the bay windows, the decorative millwork trim.

Pl. 9

At 1130 East 50th Street, set far back in a deep lot, stands one of the first Kenwood houses. Ezra Brainerd built it for his fiancée in 1867, with his mustering-out pay from the Union army. He and his wife did not stay in this house very long, moving to Woodlawn Avenue a few years later. Like so many others, he invested heavily in real estate in the Kenwood area.

Even though these houses represent but a small fraction of those that we know existed in 1871, the way they are placed on their lots hints at the differences in land use between what were already coming to be three separate communities. The South Park houses have shallow lawns, and although the lots are large, the houses are not very widely separated. The cottages in Hyde Park Center between 53d and 55th are on very small lots, built close together. In Kenwood, the 50th Street house is set deep into the property, far from the street, and hidden among trees. In general, in all three neighborhoods, lot sizes tended to be smallest close to the Illinois Central stations. "Three minutes from the depot" was a prime come-on used by developers and real estate agents to attract commuters. Proximity to the station meant that one did not have to keep a horse, and so the lot need only be large enough for a house and small yard. As the walking distance to the station increased, lots had to be larger to accommodate barns and coach houses. This was particularly true in Kenwood, which was said to have the finest array of carriages and sleighs meeting the evening train of any Chicago suburb. In this way were class differences between various localities dramatized.

The differences in land use became accentuated with the passing years as Paul Cornell's suburb took off on its own. When Chicago burned, Hyde Park–Kenwood was ready to receive a new influx: there were a number of interested developers, a local government was functioning, public works were under way, and it was attracting its own labor force. Particular areas were developing individualities of their own which would make them attractive to a broad range of people seeking homes.

2 *Years of Growth*
1872–89

The verve, optimism, and civic pride that had energized Chicago's first forty years were already in evidence as the flames of the fire died down and the ashes cooled. Her citizens, reeling under their losses and the burden of relief work, nevertheless plunged into rebuilding their city. The whole nation watched with awe as Chicago began to rise again, and her population, as before, swelled annually.

Interest in real estate south of the city was stimulated by the urgent demand for housing, resumption of work on the South Parks (although on a more modest scale under the supervision of H. W. S. Cleveland), the availability of rail service, and the opportunity outside the city limits of building frame houses. Although home building was going forward on the North Side during this period, many men who worked downtown preferred to avoid the rush-hour carriage congestion that inevitably occurred when the bridge over the Chicago River swung around to let ships through.

Fig. 7

The area we now call Hyde Park–Kenwood was developing its own very separate identity within Hyde Park Township. To the south vigorous industrial centers were growing up in Grand Crossing and around the newly opened Calumet Harbor and its docks. The flames and smoke of the mills and foundries made the southern skies crimson and black. To the west, the Union Stock Yards, established in 1865 at the heart of a network of railroads, attracted thousands of immigrant workers. Its presence, too, was felt, when the wind from the west brought in its heavy stench. Hyde Park–Kenwood was billed in the real estate ads as "exclusive" and "elegant." To the geographic separation was added a feeling of class separation, a feeling that increased in intensity as labor problems mounted in the industrial areas.

Building a community is no small task. Amenities and protective services must be provided, and problems of representation and administration solved, all in a setting of constant growth stimulated by the leavening of real estate speculation. During the years between the fire and annexation, the people of Hyde Park–Kenwood grappled with these problems, built

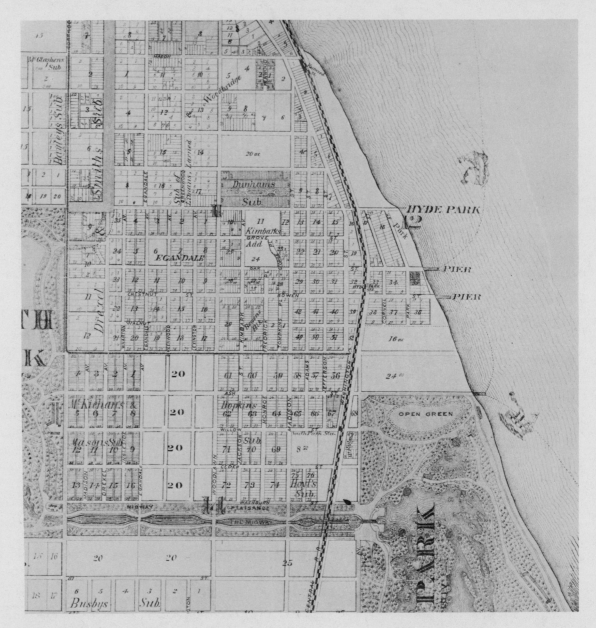

Fig. 7. Hyde Park–Kenwood in 1871. (Map courtesy of the Chicago Historical Society)

up a local economy, and created a rich and varied social life. As in any example of growth, diversity and specialization developed; the result was three separate but interrelated neighborhoods, Kenwood, Hyde Park Center, and South Park. The existing houses from these years yield evidence of the patterns of community development, the local architecture reflecting what was happening during this period.

Providing Amenities and Protective Services

In 1872 an act of the state legislature gave Hyde Park Township a "village" government, as defined by the state constitution. This is a confusing term, for ordinarily "village" suggests a small, intimate settlement. In this case, however, "village" applied to the whole of Hyde Park Township. The village government that was instituted added to the existing township officers a board of six trustees, elected for two-year terms. Three trustees were elected each year. They named their own president and appointed all the other officers except the clerk and the assessor.[1] During the seventies and eighties these trustees attacked the problems of developing the physical amenities of the village.

Within the city of Chicago during these years the fear of disease was acute, and justifiably so. Cholera, diptheria, smallpox, and scarlet fever epidemics broke out with terrifying regularity. One of the reasons people chose to leave the city was to escape these perils. Therefore, a primary preoccupation of the citizenry of Hyde Park was the provision of an adequate supply of pure drinking water and a good sewerage and draining system.

Initially, water had been obtained from wells and cisterns, and from the carts of hawkers peddling lake water. Early in the seventies a pumping station was built at the foot of 68th Street and water was supplied through a sixteen-inch pipe laid on the floor of the lake. The pipeline went west on 68th Street and supplied both Hyde Park and Lake townships, but this was not an entirely satisfactory system because the two townships had developed in such different ways. By 1879 it became clear that Lake was using nine times as much water as Hyde Park, and the question arose of how it should be paid for. As the *Tribune* commented, Hyde Park supplied the South Parks and residences, but Lake furnished the Union Stock Yards, the car shops of the Lake Shore and Rock Island railroads, and thirty packing and rendering companies.[2] The water usage figures give some indication of the differences in the quality of life in the two areas. The Village of Hyde Park at that time was reported to supply 992 houses, as against Lake's 1,637; but Hyde Park had 376 bathtubs, whereas Lake had 55; and Hyde Park had 384 toilets, as compared with Lake's 28. An agreement was reached whereby Hyde Park would pay 18.77 per cent of the water bill, Lake 81.23 per cent.[3]

Within a year, however, the Hyde Park trustees concluded that the water supply was inadequate, particularly in view of the swift industrial developments in South Chicago around Calumet Harbor, where, in addition to the iron works, lumber yards, and blast furnaces, George Pullman was just beginning to build his model town for the Pullman Palace Car Company.[4] The Hyde Park trustees determined to build their own pumping station. By 1882 contracts had been let for the new waterworks. The plan was to dig a tunnel five feet in diameter, forty-five feet under the bottom of the lake, an ambitious and difficult engineering enterprise, but one not without precedent.[5] Chicago had completed just such a tunnel in 1869, to the wonder and admiration of the whole world. With the completion of this new tunnel and the establishment of a new crib, a mile from the 68th Street shore, Hyde Park Village felt assured of an abundant supply of pure water. But within a very few years, this expensive new system was found to be unsatisfactory. Hyde Park used the lake for sewage disposal, and one mile out was not far enough to escape this kind of contamination. By 1889 the water was again full of fetid matter. Furthermore, the demand for water was so great that the pressure was often inadequate to raise it to the second floor of Hyde Park houses.[6] This feebleness of pressure drew scathing public comment when, at the dedication of the Hyde Park Methodist Church, the water-powered organ gave out in the middle of the offertory.

Drainage and sewerage presented massive problems, both in the larger village and within Hyde Park–Kenwood. Much of Hyde Park–Kenwood was marshy and muddy. Streets were ditched on either side for drainage. Many houses were built on high brick or stone foundations to lift them well above the mire and protect them from flooding. Wooden sidewalks, too, were raised; the space beneath them provided hiding places for children and nesting sites for rabbits.[7] The sewer system evolved gradually as each new area was developed; main lines were laid on 51st Street, 53d Street, and Greenwood Avenue, with feeder systems leading into them.

Each year new roads were macadamized, at considerable cost to the village. In 1878 an ordinance was passed to compel all able-bodied males between twenty-one and fifty to work on the streets for not more than three days in each year or to pay in default of that a sum of $1.25 per day.[8] This was apparently an effort to equalize the burden of paying for streets, distributing it among both owners and tenants. Sidewalks were paid for by individual owners or developers.

As a result of all this activity, the trustees of Hyde Park Village in 1887 could proudly report that there were 72 miles of macadamized streets (exclusive of park roads), 150 miles of wooden sidewalks, 6½ miles of stone sidewalks, 77 miles of water pipes, and 33 miles of sewers. The streets were lighted by 867 gas lamps and 680 oil lamps.[9]

As might be expected, with the growth of population came an increase in the need for fire and police protection. At first fires were put out by groups of neighbors passing buckets. By

Fig. 8

Fig. 9

Fig. 8. Hyde Park Waterworks, 1882–83. (Map courtesy of the Chicago Historical Society)

Fig. 9. Hyde Park drainage and sewerage, 1882–83. (Map courtesy of the Chicago Historical Society)

1875 the public waterworks permitted use of direct high-pressure service at the hydrants, obtained by increasing the speed of the pumping-station engine. This obviated the need for steam fire engines. All that was necessary was a horse-drawn hose cart and hook-and-ladder equipment. A volunteer fire department was organized with three stations, one to the north in Oakland, one in Hyde Park Center, and one at the corner of 50th and State streets.[10] This system, too, soon proved insufficient to meet the needs of the population. The stations were too far apart and the areas served too large for the volunteers to get to fires in time.

The growing population (from 3,644 in 1870 to 15,724 in 1880) also meant an increase in the number of constables employed by the village. By 1880 the police department had twenty-two officers and men; in 1883 it was decided to introduce telephone service in the form of call boxes for the police and fire departments. By 1884 the police force was up to forty men, and it continued to grow annually. The 1887 report of the chief of police recorded a marked increase in labor troubles: a Pullman strike, the Calumet Iron and Steel Company strike, and the Lake Shore and Michigan Southern switchmen's strike. By 1899, the police force totaled 104 men, and its chief recommended that even more be hired the following year. By that time the population had reached 74,000.

When we compare the police reports of 1881 and 1889, we see that in practically all areas the number of offenses was rising: arrests for disorderly conduct went from 300 to 1,237 (this undoubtedly included labor disorders); for drunk and disorderly conduct, from 96 to 127; for nude bathing, from 9 to 24; and for shooting on Sunday, from 9 to 34. The value of property stolen rose from $3,142 to $10,277, total fines from $1,873 to $11,336.[11] As the population quadrupled, so did the amount of crime, and the officers and trustees faced a massive administrative problem.

The village trustees attempted to provide still another type of protection, passing ordinances prohibiting the sale of intoxicating liquors and creating districts in which saloons were outlawed. Although these ordinances were constantly challenged, the Illinois Supreme Court sustained their legality. Not all of the Village of Hyde Park was dry, however. The southern portion with its working-class families had saloons, and on the western boundary State Street was an almost solid line of saloons from 39th to 59th streets. The northeastern part sought to keep them out. Kenwood succeeded, as did South Park, and in Hyde Park Center the saloons were confined to the commercial strip along Lake Park Avenue.

Problems of Village Government

By 1886 the quiet little residential community pioneered by Paul Cornell and his friends had grown into a governmental monstrosity. The president of the board of trustees ruefully apologized to his colleagues for the burdens they carried. The total population of Hyde Park

Village had reached 50,000, with 750 in Kenwood (this figure includes North Kenwood, which lay between 39th and 47th streets), 4,570 in Hyde Park Center, and about 500 in South Park. That is, only about one-eighth of the total population was at the northern end.[12] The economic differences between the northern end, where the average house cost $7,000, and the southern, where it cost $2,000, were sharpening.

Many business and professional people in Kenwood and South Park felt threatened by the laboring-class population of South Chicago, Calumet, and Pullman. The struggle of the laborers, chiefly foreign-born or black, for higher wages and better working conditions was seen as endangering the American free-enterprise system and the right of every man to run his business as he wished. These same workingmen were also against the strict liquor laws so dear to the hearts of those at the northern end. John Bennett, president of the board of trustees of Hyde Park Village and a resident of South Park, expressed some of these apprehensions in a speech at his college reunion in 1884. After describing the great technological progress that had been made in the preceding thirty years, he went on to say, "It remains to be seen, however, whether the American people will successfully meet and overcome the new dangers which threaten our institutions. The liberation of 4,000,000 slaves, who were necessarily in a state of ignorance, and their investiture with the franchise of citizenship was, in itself, a severe test of the elective system. But the constant influx and easy enfranchisement of a foreign population, largely uninstructed in the theory and genesis of *our* institutions . . . threaten constant and renewed peril to the permanancy of American ideas. We are in danger of becoming daily less and less American. The foreign population of our large cities is already either in the majority or possess the political power of controlling the election. So long as this is so, American ideas are in danger of being subordinated."[13] On the other hand, the big industrialists, the owners of the rolling mills, foundries, car works, and blast furnaces, were distrusted because of their efforts to gain control of the board of trustees and of the crucial jobs of treasurer, clerk, and assessor in order to assure themselves of low taxes and low water rates. Furthermore, the burgeoning industrial area was constantly in need of improvements. The northern part of the village saw no reason why it should be taxed for work on Calumet Harbor or for bridges across the Calumet River.

From 1872 onward there were expressions of dissatisfaction with the village form of government, and annexation to Chicago was discussed. In that year a petition was circulated to submit the question of annexation to a vote of the people, but the petition failed for lack of enough signatures.[14] The matter came up again in 1873, when the *Chicago Tribune* reported schemes to annex Hyde Park, Lake View, Jefferson, and all other suburban towns.[15] And early in 1876 the *Tribune* reported of Hyde Park that "the immense size of the village and the diversity of interests of the different districts have been recognized for some time as a fruitful source of embarrassment in the management of its affairs, and a movement to reorganize under the General Law as a city has been suggested as a remedy, as each portion would then elect its own representative, and many of the difficulties of the present form of municipal government would then be removed."[16] A month later the *Tribune* again commented, "The talk of reorganizing as a city with wards, aldermen, and other expensive luxuries is growing in favor." The article went on to point out that the rapid rise of the manufacturing population at the south end presented a threat to interests of the wealthy population at the north end. Because the whole village voted for the trustees, the southern members could dominate.[17]

The differences in voter viewpoints found expression in the formation of political parties. Although the Hyde Park Republican party was not formally affiliated with the national party, many of its members were. The party stressed fiscal conservatism and low taxes on industry.[18] A Citizen's party, formed in the seventies, represented the workingmen of South Chicago and the Calumet area and attempted to rally the south against the north. Their efforts to secure three of the six trusteeships stimulated the formation of the Union Taxpayers, a party that promised to make nominations without sectional strife, allowing for one representative from the south.[19]

The difficulty of the situation was exacerbated when, in 1878, it was discovered that the treasurer of the village, a Kenwood resident, owed the village $114,032.62 and did not know what had become of the money. The revelation agitated the population from one end of Hyde Park to the other. The trustees were accused of mismanagement and extravagance. Again the question of the future form of government was raised.[20]

All through the eighties the village struggled with its organizational difficulties. The special economic interests of the large manufacturers led some to seek control of the board of trustees through dictating to their employees how they should vote. Expressions of concern about cliques, "ring rule," and machine politics were yearly accompaniments to election preparations.[21] The two parties that finally emerged (others came and went) were the Republicans,[22] who ran a straight Republican ticket, and the Citizen's (or Taxpayer's), who claimed to nominate the best man regardless of party.[23] Beneath the stream of accusations of mismanagement and sometimes malfeasance ran the realization that the form of government was inappropriate, and there was endless debate over what the alternative might be.

There were those who believed that the area should be divided into three separate villages: Hyde Park, South Chicago, and Pullman. Each village would be more homogeneous, more easily managed, and their very different interests would be more fairly served. Petitions for this solution failed, however, to get the necessary approval from the state legislature.[24]

Those in favor of a city government pointed out that Hyde Park Village was already greater in territory than Chicago; a city government would be more democratic, as each ward would have its own representative; there would be no opportunity for one ring or clique to gain control of the trusteeships and other offices. Arguing against city government were those who feared bureaucracy, thought the creation of numerous jobs and agencies would inevitably lead to graft and corruption, and were apprehensive about the effect of city government on taxes. Although a petition for a referendum on the issue was drawn up, it failed for lack of signatures.[25]

Annexation

Finally, there was the solution of annexation. Initially, many were against it. Some, like George Pullman, feared it would mean higher taxes. Others, and Pullman was included in this group too, were reluctant to sacrifice their autonomy. In the latter camp were also those who wanted to maintain an independent school system and those who wished to preserve the Hyde Park liquor laws.

Heavy pressure for annexation came from Chicago itself. The *Tribune*, a Republican paper, took a strong stand for it: northern Hyde Park contained many wealthy, loyal Republicans, and drawing them into the city could only add to Republican strength. Moreover, Chicago's boosters and businessmen dreamed of elbowing out Philadelphia and becoming the second largest city in the United States by the time of the 1890 census. And in Hyde Park those who felt themselves dragged down by repeated demands for special assessments, for increases in the police force, a better fire department, more street lights, yet another new water system, looked forward to the advantages of city amenities and utilities paid for out of the general fund. Leaders assured them that their taxes would not be raised, that their liquor laws would not be altered, that the fire-ordinance limits would not be extended, and that they would at last be freed from the threat of domination by laborers and industrialists to the south. The businessmen who worked in the city gave Chicago their loyalty and believed that being a part of it could only raise property values.

The Chicago Consolidation and Annexation Bill, passed by the state legislature in 1887, provided a means for the three separate townships which comprised the city of Chicago— South Town, North Town, and West Town—to annex adjacent territories if a sufficient number of citizens of those territories petitioned and voted for annexation. Prominent Hyde Parkers, among them several who had been in the first wave (but not including Paul Cornell, who favored a city government) mounted a campaign to petition for annexation. In the spring elections of 1887 the northern portion of Hyde Park Village voted with South Town (Chicago's First, Second, Third, Fourth, and Fifth wards) for annexation. Pullman did not join, nor did Kensington, Riverdale, or Rosedale.[26]

This popular vote solved nothing. Instead it raised very real problems. How would such a large territory be represented in the city council? What was to happen to the part of Hyde Park Village that had not been annexed? How would it be governed? What should be done about the village's indebtedness? The village attorney suggested that the annexation law was so crude, contained so many uncertainties, and affected such important property interests that the trustees should retain additional lawyers to go into the matter. There was some grumbling about the lawyers being hired at village expense, but hired they were. The annexation law was tested in the Illinois Supreme Court and found invalid, and the election was declared void.[27]

The court found that the amendments to the General Law of 1872 embodied in the Consolidation and Annexation Act were unconstitutional. The court stated that the union of Hyde Park and South Town could not have been effected without extending the jurisdiction of Chicago over both, but this was not, in fact, what the voters had voted upon. They thought they were voting to join Chicago; in reality they were only voting to join South Town.

Perhaps reflecting the ambivalence they had displayed all along, Hyde Parkers were jubilant at being set free from Chicago, and when they learned the news they celebrated with bonfires in the streets and marching bands.[28]

But the matter did not rest there. Chicago was not ready to give up its ambitious plan. The city's corporation counsel prepared a new legislative act, and while Hyde Park limped along with an increasingly uncomfortable interim government, fresh plans were laid for another vote, this time by all of Hyde Park Village, all of the people of Chicago, and three other petitioning towns, Jefferson, Lake, and Lake View.[29]

At the same time there was last-ditch agitation for a city government for Hyde Park Village, led by A. G. Proctor, publisher of the *Hyde Park Herald,* Daniel Peirce, former president of the trustees, and Henry V. Freeman, former village attorney.[30] George M. Pullman conducted his own campaign against annexation, for in this vote Pullman would be involved. The *Chicago Herald* summarized the situation by remarking, "All of Hyde Park is divided into three parties, republicans, annexationists, and George M. Pullmanites, and the difference between the first and last is as Tweedledee from Tweedledum."[31]

The people voted on June 28, 1889. Considering the amount of furor that had preceded the election, the turnout was surprisingly small: 5,212 citizens of Hyde Park Village voted for annexation, 3,357 against. The Fifth, Sixth, Seventh, and Ninth precincts, which contained what today we call Hyde Park–Kenwood, were against annexation.[32] On the following day, a

27

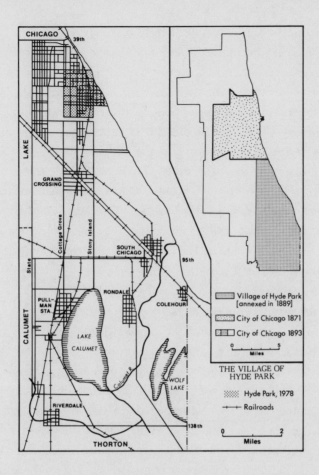

Fig. 10. The Village of Hyde Park in 1889, the year of annexation.

Fig. 10

Saturday, the *Tribune* optimistically announced that "Sunday's Sun Will Shine on One United City, Second Only to New York." And indeed on that day Chicago added 130 square miles to her territory.

In July the *Tribune* described the new jewel in Chicago's crown. A trip through Hyde Park was full of interest and novelty to the visitor, who could go by the Cottage Grove Avenue cable cars, or charter a small steamer or yacht and sail along the lakeshore, disembarking at the old pier at the foot of 53d Street, always populated with men or boys fishing. "There is a main village street in Hyde Park with neat stores, but in the day time it is almost as quiet as a lane in a country churchyard." In the evening, "when Hyde Parkers return, it brightens up; ... many promenaders are out on the well-kept stone walks; a lawn party is seen here and there; gay turn-outs and family equipages roll over the boulevards." The residents "possess many advantages that the city resident does not. For one thing, rents are cheaper; the air seems purer; they appear to take a deeper more neighborly interest in each other; they meet on the trains going into town in the morning and again upon going home in the evening; after having traversed every section and encountered multitudinous interests during the day they compare notes, like an army of scouts who have spied out the land. They are great readers of newspapers and generally well-informed upon all public affairs and subjects of interest; . . . the new portion of Chicago is a mass of green all over, great shade trees of maple, ash, and locust lining all the wide streets and avenues."[33]

Thus, in twenty-five years the little prairie settlement came to be adjoined as a prosperous and desirable appendage to the city of Chicago. The changes that had taken place since its inception did not go unnoted, however; John D. Sherman, son of the second man to settle in Kenwood, Pennoyer Sherman, wrote wistfully, "My village? When I moved in there wasn't any. While I lived there it grew to be the biggest in the world, both in extent of territory and population. And though I still live within a block of where I moved in, there isn't any more village now than there was then, and I'm only 32 years old . . . .

"Maybe it was because there were so many ponies hitched to that barnyard fence that the quail quit nesting in the old place and the rabbits didn't seem to like our hazel bushes any more, and the wild pigeons didn't stop to rest in our big oaks, and the spring beauties, and pinks, and prairie flowers, and lady slippers, and daisies kind of got fewer every year. Or maybe lake water, and gas, and paved streets, and electric lights, and taxes had something to do with it. At any rate, the birds,—sparrows don't count—and the rabbits, and the flowers are all gone—and the boys too. And so is Hyde Park."[34]

Five years after annexation Laura Willard, a graduate student at the new University of Chicago, wrote an introduction to a never completed master's thesis on the history of Hyde Park: "It is the omnivorous spirit of the modern city, devouring all that lies before it, which takes the place of the death-angel and restores to the municipality its analogy to the life of a man. The outlying village may have been quite independent in its beginnings; it may have epitomized within itself the political struggles, the mistakes and successes of a nation. But when swallowed by the hungry city, it has practically ceased to live. Like the human life which is said to have vanished, it has been absorbed by a larger whole." In a footnote she observed that the very name seemed to disappear. The Hyde Park cars on the Cottage Grove line were replaced by others saying Jackson Park; Hyde Park Center on the Illinois Central became 53d Street. The Hyde Park Police Station became that of the Tenth Precinct, and the Hyde Park Post Office vanished: "Not only, however, can Hyde Park scarcely any longer be said to have so much as 'a name to live'; its very tombstone is already erected! Behold it in the 'Station N' which replaces the familiar legend in the former addresses of Hyde Park residents. What is Station N, or X, or Y, or Z—to her whose glory has departed?"[35]

Laura Willard's mournful little metaphor may have seemed a valid portent at the time. But, as it turned out, Hyde Park did not die. It was not swallowed by the city and did not lose its sense of community. There are many reasons for this, some of which can be found in the following decade, some much later, deep into the twentieth century. It might be appropriate, however, to look at Hyde Park–Kenwood as it evolved between 1871 and 1889 to see what it had that contributed to its durability.

Searching back to discover how the northern part of Hyde Park Village grew and shaped itself, a number of physical, social, economic, and psychological determinants seem to emerge.

The Physical Scene

Geographically it was encapsulated: the city on the north, the lake on the east, the parks on the south, and the boulevards to the west formed firm boundaries. Hyde Park–Kenwood could not be reached from the West Side by any form of public transportation. It is doubtful if many people living west of Cottage Grove Avenue ever saw its much-touted lakefront, Jackson Park (so named in 1881), or the boulevards. Woodlawn, with the exception of a few scattered houses, including that of James Wadsworth at 63d Street and Woodlawn Avenue, was a vast prairie; the 60th Street Illinois Central Station did not open until 1888. To the north and west lay a crescent of institutions: the Reform School, the Home for the Friendless, the Erring Woman's Refuge, and the Home for Incurables, so placed on the assumption that isolation and fresh air were the best things for the pitiable.

Within this charmed circle the physical assets—the transportation, the lake, and the parklands—drew and held people. The transportation was constantly being modernized and made more efficient.

Gone were the little wood-burning trains that, to the delight of residents, had scurried across the horizon, like domestic pets. The excessive demand for fuel and lumber soon depleted the Wisconsin and Michigan forests, and the Illinois Central converted to coal. In 1879 the Illinois Central graded its roadbed and laid new suburban tracks, made specially in England and shipped via New Orleans.[36] The new tracks enabled the Illinois Central to run suburban trains every half-hour during the day.[37] The locomotives had headlights and pilots ("cowcatchers") at each end, so they never had to turn around. The cable car that supplanted the steam dummy on 55th Street in 1887 was cleaner, quieter, and faster than its predecessor. The boulevards laid out by Olmsted and Vaux offered a scenic route for carriages from the downtown area to the South Parks, while also providing highly fashionable residential sites.

The lake, of course, was an important attraction. Bathing was popular and informal. Boating was a favorite community sport. A forty-foot, eight-oared barge purchased by the

Kenwood Barge Club was housed in a boathouse built on one of the Illinois Central piers at 53d Street and Lake Park Avenue. The land had been eroded by the lake to form a good harbor where East End Park is now and the shore under the bluff was lined with boathouses. On pleasant evenings as many as fifty, or even a hundred, boats would cluster for community singing.[38]

The parks and parkways were heavily used and fastidiously maintained. Their gardeners, English, German, Scandinavian, trained in the old country, created fantastic displays of flowers, not only in conventional borders, but in the shapes of animal and human figures. Woodland walks were carefully tended. Open grassy spaces were cropped by wandering flocks of sheep. In summer the lagoons were used for boating, in winter for ice skating and curling. Thousands of people attended the concerts in Washington Park, and the new pavilion in Jackson Park offered a breezy lakeside setting for parties and dances on summer nights.

The Social Life

Socially, the people who lived in Hyde Park–Kenwood took part in both a city life and a suburban life. But the two were different. During its suburban period before annexation, people in Hyde Park–Kenwood, particularly the wealthier ones, participated in and contributed to the formal city life with its business and professional organizations, its large cultural institutions such as the Historical Society, the Art Institute, and the symphony orchestra, its philanthropies, its great balls and benefits. Locally, social life was more informal and diverse, shared by men and women and their families. A number of interests were served; groups were formed for community betterment, self-improvement, entertainment, or all three.

Political meetings were well attended. In addition to the Republican and Citizen's parties there was an active local chapter of the Irish Land League, an Irish nationalist organization, which met at Lynch's Hall on 55th Street.[39] Church members worked together to raise building funds, establish Sunday schools, and open missions, both in this country and in faraway lands. Among the numerous cultural organizations was the Mendelssohn Club, which had a membership of about 150 persons, including many exceptionally fine musicians. Its director was Frederick W. Root, and its pianist Miss Jessie Root. The concerts were ambitious, including such works as the oratorio *Elijah*.[40] The Shakespeare Club met regularly in the homes of its members, giving Restoration as well as Shakespearean plays. The Hyde Park Philosophical Society also met in the homes of its members, who presented for discussion papers on subjects of current interest such as "Modern Socialist Experiments," "The Duty of the Citizen to the High School," "Heredity," "Sanitary Problems," and "Natural Gas."

The Hyde Park Lyceum, a locally sponsored community library, had reading rooms in

Flood's Hall on 53d Street.[41] It, too, had programs that drew upon the expertise of people who lived in the neighborhood. One such person was the architect Louis Sullivan, a Kenwood resident, who gave a talk about the Auditorium Building in 1889, just one month before it opened.

New clubs sprang up constantly. The Kenwood Club was formed in the seventies, meeting in members' homes. By the mid-eighties it had its own social center in the old Judd house at 47th Street and Lake Park Avenue, with a dancing hall, reading room, reception parlors, smoking room, and billiard hall.[42] The Home Circle gave parties in Flood's Hall; the Kenwood Dramatic Club gave plays; the South Park Club, similar to the Kenwood Club, had a clubhouse at 57th and Harper, complete with gymnasium, bowling alleys, and social rooms.[43]

Tennis, introduced from England in 1874, was played on the four private courts of the Kenwood Club, and by 1886 both Washington and Jackson parks had public courts.[44] And there were the bicycle clubs. The bicycle craze was not without its complications. Horses shied, pedestrians were terrified, as the first cyclists wobbled or whizzed down the quiet village streets.[45] Baseball had been popular even before the fire, which temporarily cut short the career of the White Stockings. After the fire they were reorganized, and A. G. Spaulding produced a championship team in the National League.[46] The fact that A. G. Spaulding lived in Kenwood and was an active member of the Kenwood Club could only have heightened interest in the triumphs of the White Stockings.

The great spectator sport, however, was horse racing. The Washington Park Club, which occupied eighty acres at 61st Street and Grand Boulevard (now King Drive) drew members from all over the city. Built in 1883 by Solon S. Beman, it had the most elegantly appointed clubhouse and the finest race course in the United States, some said in the world. Its grandstand could seat ten thousand people, and the club itself contained parlors, private and public dining rooms, sleeping rooms, and observatories said to be of unsurpassed richness and beauty. All of the rooms and halls had fireplaces especially designed by Beman. Members from every part of Chicago could reach it easily, their smart carriages rolling down Drexel and Grand boulevards. And visitors came from all over the United States to watch the races.[47]

The need for associations, for coming together, also found expression in women's groups. With growing prosperity and the ready availability of domestic servants, made possible by the tide of immigrants surging into Chicago, middle-class women found themselves with a new freedom and a new leisure. But many of them were also very isolated. In Kenwood, in particular, but also to some extent in South Park, the wealthier one was the farther one was likely to live from the center of activity. Women who lived on 47th or 48th streets and

Drexel, Ellis, or Greenwood avenues were a long way from the shopping area at 53d and Lake Park. These were also the women whose husbands were involved in Chicago's civic activities, so it is not surprising to see them form their own groups, both citywide and local. In 1873, Mrs. Charles Hitchcock, of Kenwood, helped found the Fortnightly Club, the first women's club in Chicago. Other women in Hyde Park–Kenwood soon joined her in the group, which was devoted to serious study and discussion.[48] Founded in 1876, the Chicago Woman's Club had as its object "mutual sympathy and counsel and united effort toward the higher civilization of humanity." At first its chief activities were study classes in art and literature, and it described itself as the "mature woman's college," but in time its interests broadened to include philanthropy and social action. Its membership was drawn from all parts of the city and suburbs and included many Hyde Park–Kenwood women, both as participants and as leaders. Emily Nolan, of Drexel Boulevard, was one of the leaders. She formed the Society for the Promotion of Physical Culture and Correct Dress, a group that sought to reform women's clothing and free women from the slavery of fashion.[49]

The plight of other women who were without financial support was a matter of continuing concern. In 1887 Mrs. Jonathan Y. Scammon helped to form the Chicago Society of Decorative Art and became its first president. The purpose of the society was to help "needy gentlewomen" learn to support themselves by working in the decorative arts. Eventually it found quarters in the old Art Institute building at Michigan and Van Buren. It not only took orders for needlework, painting, and sculpture for various churches, clubs, and private homes but helped find regular employment for its graduates. A number of Hyde Park–Kenwood women served on its board.[50] In the late eighties the Arché Club and the Travel Club were formed to study and encourage the fine arts.

A local group, the Union Charitable Society, composed of representatives of all the churches in the community, was formed to help poor women whose husbands were sick, unemployed, or deceased. In 1884 the society handled fifty cases of destitution and sickness, established a sewing school for forty-seven pupils, and began to work for a kindergarten in connection with the public schools. They delivered Christmas dinners to every needy family and distributed coal during the cold weather. Their well-meaning if sometimes insensitive approach was epitomized in the suggestion that a large blackboard be set up in one of the stores in Hyde Park and the names of all those in want of work, as well as those in need of servants of any kind, be kept on the board.[51]

Working for women at the state level was Catharine V. Waite, who, with her husband Charles, had been in the first group to settle in Hyde Park Center. Both Waites joined with Myra Bradwell to found the Illinois Woman Suffrage Association in the early seventies.[52] In 1872, to call public attention to the women's rights issue, Catharine Waite and her daughter attempted to register to vote. When they were turned away, her husband brought suit. The judge in the case turned out to be none other than John Jameson, former partner of Charles Waite and Paul Cornell, now a judge of the Superior Court of Chicago. He ruled that "in this state a woman cannot vote, that there is no claim of Divine right to the elective franchise. This government is one of representation, and the Constitution of the United States has declared that this representation shall be through male citizens, . . . the male being selected to represent the will of the houshold."[53]

Undeterred, Catharine Waite continued to work for women's rights. In the eighties she enrolled in the Union College of Law (later Northwestern Law School), and was admitted to the bar in 1886. She inaugurated and published the quarterly *Chicago Law Times* which discussed the legal rights of women and legal aspects of insanity, abortion, and divorce. In 1888 she was elected president of the International Women's Bar Association.[54]

Catharine Waite was not the only woman in the area to achieve professional status. Her daughter Lucy was the first woman graduated from the old University of Chicago to go to medical school.[55] Other woman doctors who practiced in the community were Alice Ewing and Kate Graves. Helen Starrett, lecturer and journalist, was the editor of *Western Magazine,* and later head of the Starrett School.

In sum, the available evidence seems to indicate that the local life encouraged the expression of a wide variety of recreational, cultural, social, and intellectual interests. The abundant associations and opportunities for social interplay created strong bonds between people, so that even when Hyde Park–Kenwood became a part of Chicago it continued to think of itself as separate and special. The feeling of community membership was reinforced by the fact that the oldest residents continued to play a part in the various associations, giving them an air of stability unusual at a time when mobility seemed to prevail.

The Local Economy

With the political, physical, and social development of the neighborhood came economic development as well, but of a very different sort from that of many middle western small towns. In a sense, the business of Hyde Park–Kenwood was that of building itself; the economy of the community rested entirely on purveying goods and services, real estate transactions, and home building. This, too, may have contributed to its durability, for although there were fluctuations in the real estate market and building activity, such an economy was not subject to the depradations that resulted from changes in technology or the disappearance of markets—ills that affected towns built around particular industries or services. On the contrary, the recurrent demand for real estate and housing outside the central city assured a continual growth, albeit one that sometimes slackened during periods of depression.

A comparison of the classified pages of the first and last years of the *Hyde Park Directory*, 1883 and 1889, shows the phenomenal development of goods and services. The first cluster of stores at 53d and Lake Park had been augmented in the seventies by the Flood Block on 53d Street, a two-story building containing several small stores and two large halls that were used for meetings and social gatherings. During the eighties the number of shops on Lake Park Avenue increased from forty-two to sixty-nine, and thirty-three new shops opened on 53d Street between Lake Park and Harper, beginning an encroachment on what had been a residential street. On 55th Street, also residential, and on the cable car line, twenty-two new shops were opened between Lake Park and Kimbark by 1889. In South Park a small shopping area of about seven stores was erected on 57th Street between Harper and Blackstone avenues.

During these years the number of food stores grew from six to forty, including several of a new kind: two bakers, seven fruit and confectionery shops, five milk depots, a caterer, and a popcorn maker. Five cigar and tobacco shops appeared. Blacksmiths, wagon- and carriage-makers, livery stables, and harnessmakers also increased in number. The growing self-sufficiency of the community is indicated by the rise in the number of tailors, dressmakers, boot and shoe stores, and dry goods stores, as well as the presence of a community newspaper and a news agency. With this rise in goods and services we can assume a proportionate increase in the population of shopkeepers and artisans, most of whom lived above or behind their stores. The inference drawn from the census of 1870 that the land between 53d and 55th streets was developing into an area of working-class homes seems to be borne out by the presence on Lake Park Avenue of two billiard halls and eight saloons, the laborer's equivalent of the Kenwood and South Park Clubs.

That there was also a marked rise in the number of professional people is apparent from the listings of dentists and doctors. Five dentists had opened offices in the neighborhood by 1889, and nineteen physicians and surgeons. It is noteworthy that only one physician also had an office downtown. Again, this seems to indicate a growing self-sufficiency, as well as a population large enough and affluent enough to support these services.

During this period the number of building-related services tripled; there were seventeen carpentry and building firms and four new hardware and wallpaper stores in 1889. Five local real estate offices are listed, whereas none was on record in 1883. Apparently, until this time real estate transactions took place in downtown Chicago.

Three Communities and Their Houses

One quality, intrinsic to Hyde Park–Kenwood, which might account in part for its durability was its diversity. Not that it was planned that way. Rather, the diversity was the result of the

35

untrammeled eagerness of the real estate developers to make the most on their investments. But ultimately this meant that somewhere there was a place to live for almost anyone. The result was a community that grew rather than diminished in vitality, attracting a wide variety of people.

During the eighties, although there was certainly a great deal of social contact among the three communities of Kenwood, Hyde Park Center, and South Park, differences existing from the beginning began to be accentuated. Each of the three clusters was developing its own individuality, an individuality that is still apparent in the houses remaining today.

A number of factors operated in varying degrees to determine where people built or bought houses and what kinds they selected—access to transportation, economic capability, appeals of the real estate promoters and developers, self-image and ideals for family life, and, finally, a broadening interest in domestic architecture and home decoration.

The Advance of Domestic Architecture

This awareness was fostered by the professionalization of the Chicago architects. These men were becoming concerned with their own education; they were forming associations; and they were writing and speaking for each other with interest and intensity. The Chicago school, as it later came to be called, through its innovative contributions to the construction of commercial buildings, was a powerful stimulus to local architects.

This had not always been so. W. W. Boyington, architect of the Chicago Water Tower, the only public building to survive the fire, writing in 1887, recalled that when he came to Chicago in 1853 he found that the architects then in practice were former master builders or contractors. Chicago and the West at that time could hardly be said to require the services of professional architects. The builders, who soon found that it was desirable to work from drawings, simply selected their best draftsman and paid him two dollars a day to produce plans.[56]

In the seventies *Chicago Architect and Building News* had deplored the state of domestic architecture in Chicago. "The dwelling house architecture of Chicago has always been far behind that of her business buildings . . . . Her population has always been so transient, and the spirit of speculation has been such, that no one ever thought of living long in one house or of making it a comfortable home. Every one was aspiring to a higher state; and no one felt warranted in building for permanence. The frame buildings, which were the rule—stone or brick being the exceptions—were always built with heavy sills, so they could be moved away."[57]

In the eighties, however, domestic architecture was coming to be regarded as an art which could and should express the particular dweller's individuality. A number of aesthetic and social factors probably contributed to the lively interest in domestic architecture.

One important influence was Ruskin's *Poetry of Architecture,* in which he described the architect as a metaphysician who, studying the family for whom he plans a home, must acquaint himself with the character and requirements of each member.[58] This approach fitted in nicely with the nineteenth-century ideal of a close family life around which all other activities revolved. John Root wrote of the disappearance of the stiff parlor and the pleasures of a family living room, of the importance of a large and welcoming reception room for friends who come to call.

He also pointed out that the residential architecture of the West (meaning west of Boston and New York) was unique. Western cities were not as dense as those of the East. Eastern cities were begun when "their citizens were more interdependent and facilities for transportation were less complete than they are now." There were more detached western houses, with more trees and ground around them. Furthermore, the suburban effect was enhanced by the extraordinary increase in available materials, which, combined with the western love of novelty, often led to the erection of houses as different as possible in material, color, and treatment, all on the same street. There was none of the monotony so characteristic of eastern cities. There was a wholesome reaction toward more simple and honest buildings. Western houses were more open, there were more windows. They were larger, and the interior spaces flowed more freely.[59] Above all, the houses expressed their owners.[60]

Francis Le Baron and others extolled the fireplace and the open fire as the soul of the living room, drawing the household around it in cozy chat.[61] Irving Pond developed the idea of the American home designed by the sympathetic architect as "the highest type of home, a democratic home where love rules," and from which no evil can spring.[62] And George Maher wrote of the uniqueness of the American home, free from the strictures of rule and style of European dwellings, honest in construction and supremely comfortable.[63]

There was a new exuberance and a new sensitivity in designing domestic architecture that had heretofore shown itself only in the homes built for the very wealthy. This feeling on the part of the architects was fed by the general public's increasing awareness of the power of the decorative arts and of architecture to enhance life. In the introduction to a *Sketch Book of the Exposition of 1883,* we are told, "Everywhere and in everything is seen a desire to beautify and display the accumulations of wealth resulting from abundant business."

The exposition, which had been held annually since 1873 in a vast building designed by W. W. Boyington (on the site of the present Art Institute) is described as a fairyland of lights, music, playing fountains, and fluttering flags. In addition to such marvels as the Wilson

Sewing Machine and the Remington Type-Writing Machine, there were displays of furniture and building materials. The exposition is pictured for the reader by a fictional trio of young people who have come to spend the day. One of them remarks on the differences in the architecture of the day from that of about ten years ago, and he exhorts his friends to "observe the perfect elegance of the ornate business structures here in Chicago, and especially of the suburban residences. Those of recent design are *all* beautiful; in fact, as a rule they may be described as works of art. Their picturesque effect is really quite fascinating: such charming doorways, beautiful windows, surprising gables, and grand chimneys!"[64]

And even the *Hyde Park Herald* noted that "suburban housing has been reformed from the large bay-window box of a house to tasty cottages and Queen Anne residences."[65]

An array of new materials was available, among them stained glass, growing in use so that no moderately elegant residence or building was considered complete without it. From the stained glass imported from Italy or Germany in large tinted sheets, four establishments in Chicago designed and made windows, doors, screens, bookcase panels, and fire screens.[66] Francis Le Baron, writing in *Inland Architect* in July 1884, tell us: "Time out of mind stained glass has been used as ornament. It has added a grace to architecture, a solemnity to religions, and has vibrated in harmony with the highest note struck by gaiety and pleasure . . . . Its purple radiance pours through royal houses, and the humble household has its brightly tinted window, at sight of which the baby laughs and claps its hands, and reaches from its cradle or from its mother's arms to grasp the shining treasure."[67]

Copper for roofing was used increasingly, not only because of a decline in price but because it was more durable than tin, and grew more beautiful with time.[68] Terra cotta was gaining favor as a material for decorative use, being cheaper than stone and easily preformed. Clay for terra cotta had been found near Chicago, and manufacturers went to England to perfect their methods. They brought back not only new methods, but samples, designs, and photographs.[69] The fluidity of design made possible by the use of terra cotta found its finest expression in the work of Sullivan and Elmslie, but many examples of lesser work survive in the neighborhood. At this time, too, ornamental plaster became a popular decorative material for almost all classes of interiors. It was especially favored for ceilings and fireplaces.[70] The growth of factories for making pressed brick and the development of a means of quarrying stone mechanically led to an increased use of both brick and stone.[71]

In addition to their interest in materials as such, architects' concerns extended to the solution of problems of sanitation, fireproofing, lighting, ventilating, and heating. It was a time of structural innovation, a time when new ideas, new materials, new inventions, new methods, provided the tools and the inspiration for architects: their sharing of knowledge and mutual stimulation made the period one of the most important in Chicago's architectural history.

Houses in Kenwood

We can catch the flavor of life in Kenwood, and its pattern of development before annexation, in the houses that remain from that period. Many were the victims of a continuous renewal process that took place in the latter part of the nineteenth and first decade of the twentieth century, when the older frame homes were torn down, or perhaps burned, and were replaced by "modern" brick houses. Others survived until the period of planned urban renewal in the 1950s. These included Kenwood Court, one of the earliest developments, and many large houses along Lake Park Avenue.

It is not feasible to discuss all of the existing houses built before 1890. Those described here, and in the other neighborhoods as well, both during this period and the succeeding one, were selected with three questions in mind: Is the house typical of a larger group? Is it in a good state of preservation? Is it by a well-known Chicago architect? Among those of architectural significance a further selection sometimes had to be made. This was more subjective. An effort was made to choose those houses which best exemplified the particular architect's approach.

Pl. 10   The most substantial, and probably least altered, of the houses from the seventies is the fine Italianate structure at 4812 Woodlawn, built by C. S. Bouton of the Union Foundry Works in 1873 on a large tract of land that extended all the way to 47th Street. In appearance, and in some of the interior detail, it closely resembles the Hoyt house in South Park, and with good reason, for Bouton was married to Hoyt's daughter. Hoyt's other daughter was married to Hamilton Bogue, like his father-in-law, also a real estate broker; their home, "Greenwood," just behind the Boutons, gave the street its name. The Bogues' move to Greenwood Avenue in the early seventies illustrates a kind of internal migration that was already taking place. The family had been in the first group that settled in Hyde Park Center; the move to Greenwood was yet another move "into the country."

Throughout the seventies and eighties Kenwood steadfastly maintained its reputation as an "aristocratic" residential community close to the lake and within easy reach of the suburban trains. There were no stores and no saloons. The Kenwood Club was the neighborhood meeting place.

Pl. 11   Kimbark Avenue between 47th and 49th streets offers a sampler of the houses built in the eighties. They are typically suburban, freestanding, set back on their lawns, with verandahs to offer not only shelter from the sun but a transition from indoors to outdoors, from privacy to

Pl. 12
Pl. 13

neighborliness. They were referred to as "picturesque," and their Queen Anne style offered ample opportunity for indulging individual fancies. Two architects undoubtedly influenced the development of these and neighboring houses: Reynolds Fisher, of the firm of Patton and Fisher, who built his own shingled house at 4734 Kimbark; and George A. Garnsey, the architect for 4800 Kimbark.

Garnsey, a Hyde Parker himself, was also the editor of the *National Builder,* first published in 1885. The *National Builder,* a monthly journal, was devoted to practical building. Each month it printed a complete set of working plans, specifications, and cost estimates for a specially designed house, keeping carpenters and builders in touch with the latest in house designs. Subscriptions were $3.00 a year, and individual blueprints could be ordered for another $3.00. Customers (and their contractors and builders) had a choice of country villas, suburban cottages, Eastlake, Queen Anne, Elizabethan, Russian, or rustic styles; cheap city houses, boulevard residences, or elaborate city residences. The journal was affiliated with, and indeed the spokesman for, the sash and door manufacturers. Charles Chandler, a sash and door manufacturer, was its treasurer. Each month it printed effusive letters of gratitude from all over the United States.[72]

A number of the houses on this stretch of Kimbark are pictured in a promotional brochure brought out in the eighties called "Picturesque Kenwood." A variety of materials are used: wood, slate, stucco, stone, brick. Gables, turrets, and stained-glass windows provide the ornamentation. The general air is one of quiet informality; children standing on the wooden sidewalks or beside the neat low fences gaze solemnly at the camera, as if to say that this is where they belong, in a safe, healthful, comfortable setting.

To the south, all the way to 51st Street, stretching from Dorchester to Woodlawn and including Madison Park, lay John Dunham's largely undeveloped subdivision. Although he was said to have bought this land for a summer estate, there is no evidence that he himself ever used it as such. The cottages on 50th Street (1229 and 1243) were probably built for the farmer and gardener. That he did anticipate a demand for a much denser development is indicated by his subdivision of Madison Park and 50th Street into very small city-type lots. The large greenhouse shown on *Rascher's Atlas* of 1890 at Kenwood and 49th must have been part of his estate; the florist listed there in the 1889 Hyde Park classified directory may have been his gardener, or, by that time he may have simply leased the greenhouse. Be that as it may, the apparent dual purpose of Dunham's investment was not atypical of men who bought large pieces of "country" land and held it awaiting the auspicious moment.

Kenwood houses and their surrounding grounds are larger as one moves west, away from the 47th Street depot; coach houses were a necessity. Many of these houses were designed by architects who had established reputations for building fashionable residences, or whose successful industrial and commercial buildings commended them to their clients. Daniel Burnham and John Root, for instance, built several houses (none of which remains) for men who had businesses in the stockyards. The only Burnham and Root house left in Kenwood is

Pl. 14

that built for J. H. Nolan, an insurance broker, on Drexel Boulevard. Of subtly variegated brick, with strong stone lintels emphasizing the windows, it is massively simple, particularly when compared with the Queen Anne houses on Kimbark.

Pl. 15

Typical of the castlelike, stone "boulevard house" is the gray rough-cut stone Romanesque mansion built for Martin Ryerson on Drexel by the firm of Treat and Foltz in the eighties. The son of a successful lumber merchant and heir to his fortune, Ryerson was, at the time this house was built, one of Chicago's wealthiest citizens. He retired very early from active business and devoted himself to developing Chicago's cultural and educational resources. He was instrumental in founding and nurturing the University of Chicago, the Art Institute of Chicago, and the Field Museum.

Pl. 16

Also left from the eighties is the Turner house at 4935 Greenwood Avenue, built by Solon S. Beman, the young Hyde Park architect who designed the Washington Park Club and whose lasting fame is based on his design for George Pullman's model town.

Hyde Park Center

During this period Hyde Park Center, between 51st and 55th, showed a different kind of development. Unlike Kenwood, where the railroad tracks defined the eastern boundary, in Hyde Park Center they ran through the community, dividing it into "east of the tracks" and "west of the tracks." Although the first Hyde Park House that Paul Cornell built burned in 1877, in the eighties Hyde Park Boulevard was again being developed, this time for large boulevard residences. One of the developers, A. F. Shuman, used George Maher for his architect. Maher, like Frank Lloyd Wright, had previously been employed in Joseph Silsbee's office. Like Wright, also, Maher was searching for new forms and new meaning in architectural expression. Of the four houses that he built for Shuman on Hyde Park Boulevard, two

Pls. 17, 18

remain, 5522 and 5518. The influence of Richardson's Romanesque buildings can be seen in 5522, with its heavy arched entrance and massive turrets. In 5518 we see a more individualistic and innovative expression in the composition of rough brick and creamy, delicately carved stone, the strong horizontal lines and the treatment of the first-floor windows. On this same lot, but to the west, facing on Cornell Avenue are three more houses, apparently also by Maher, built a year or so later.

On the west side of the tracks, beyond what was the commercial strip on Lake Park Avenue, is an amalgam of urban row houses, suburban villas, and workingmen's cottages. A cottage was distinguished from a villa in that it could be managed without household help. Usually a cottage did not have a separate dining room. Both cottages and villas were freestanding, unlike the row houses which had common walls.

Within three years of the fire, row-house construction had started in the vicinity of the 53d Street Station.[73] These were crammed onto small lots, designed for quick sale or rental and maximum realization on the investment. The townhouses at 5322–28 Blackstone Avenue, built in the seventies, resemble many on Chicago's West and North sides. They stand on high basements offering protection from the mud and waters of the street. In the houses at 52d and Dorchester the builder individualized the facades, a common practice among row-house builders of that period. On Blackstone Avenue the houses from 5211 to 5221 epitomize row-house economy. When they were built they were described as a remarkable achievement, for a way had been found to erect six houses on a hundred-foot lot. They were only sixteen feet wide, but they were said to contain every convenience to be found in a house of the usual size: wood mantels, dumping grates, electric bells, speaking tubes, a bathroom, a servant's room in the basement, a butler's pantry, closets in every room, and a large linen closet.[74]

A few suburban villas have survived from this period, among them 5216 Blackstone and 5146 Harper, but even as they were being built, land use around them was changing. Across the street Paul Cornell was erecting the new Hyde Park Hotel on the block between Harper and Lake Park where his home had stood.

During the seventies and eighties real estate men were aware that Chicago, fiercely determined to rebuild after the fire and the financial panic that followed, would need workingmen. They recognized that there would be a ready market for small houses. They made repeated pleas for low suburban fares so that workingmen could own their houses on less expensive property outside the fire limits. Furthermore, they argued that the workingman needed someone to buy the land, subdivide it, build cheap houses, and sell them with the lots for a little cash down and monthly payments.[75] Much of the area between Harper and Woodlawn, 53d and 55th, was subdivided into small lots to accommodate frame cottages for lower- and middle-income families, continuing a process that had started early in the community's history. A number of these cottages can still be seen on Blackstone, Dorchester, and Ridgewood Court. An interesting variant of the Chicago cottage, originally designed to be built of wood, appeared in the early eighties, when identical houses were constructed of brick. The brick cottages on Dorchester are backed by similar ones on Ridgewood Court. All of these

Pl. 19

Pl. 20
Pl. 21

Pl. 22
Pl. 23

Pl. 24

Pl. 25

simple dwellings were within a short walk of the 55th Street cable car and the Illinois Central station. The men who lived in them could work in the neighborhood, downtown, or in the mills and factories to the south.

West of Kimbark there was still a great deal of open land. A news item from the *Chicago Tribune* in January 1884 about a fire in the stable of B. F. Ayer, general solicitor of the Illinois Central, reveals something about the land use in this area as well as the problems Hyde Park Village had in providing adequate services for such an extensive community. After the fire broke out in the Ayer stable at 52nd and Drexel, a group of volunteers tried to put it out, for it was impossible for the village fire company to get there in time from the Oakland Station. The volunteers were not able to save the barn, but they did save the house, two of the horses, two cows and a calf, three carriages, and a sleigh.[76]

South Park

South Park, during this period, was far less densely populated than Hyde Park Center. Lots were bigger, although few were as large as those in Kenwood. With the exception of the J. Y. Scammons' "Fernwood," on 59th Street between Dorchester and Woodlawn, the Daniel Shorey house on Woodlawn between 55th and 56th, and J. Frank Aldrich's estate on 57th Street between Blackstone and Harper, most of the residences were comfortable middle- and upper-middle-class dwellings, attractive but not pretentious.

On Harper Avenue, between 57th and 59th, Rosalie Villas were named for Rosalie Buckingham, who some years later married Harry Gordon Selfridge, general manager of Marshall Field and Company and subsequently founder of Selfridge's in London. In the latter part of 1883 Miss Buckingham bought these two blocks and subdivided them for forty-two villas and cottages. The plan was for each site to have a forty-five- to fifty-foot frontage, each house to be detached, and a uniform building line established. There were to be no alleys, as every lot would be wide enough to have a driveway on one side to reach the stable in the rear. There were to be sixty feet between the houses on the east side and the railroad tracks, which the railroad company was expected to landscape in harmony with the general plan. Because the trains at that time ran at ground level, the houses looked out on the park lagoons and the lake. F. R. Chandler, Rosalie Buckingham's brother-in-law, and a real estate investor, was a partner in this enterprise.

In practice, there were some modifications in the original plans. Although many of the sites did have forty-five- to fifty-foot frontages, a number of them were built on twenty-five-foot lots. The smaller houses did not have driveways or stables. Even the stipulation that all the houses be detached was violated by Solon S. Beman's double house for J. J. Jackman, Jr.

Pl. 26

All of the houses were erected under Beman's supervision. Rosalie Villas were to emulate, on a miniature scale, Beman's planned town of Pullman, a complete manufacturing center with carworks, churches, schools, market, hotel, water tower, and 1,300 houses for employees. The Rosalie Villas plan included, in addition to the residences, all of which were to be architecturally unique and in the picturesque style, a business block with a drugstore, family grocery store, cafe, club, reading room, and a public hall for lectures and concerts.

As Hyde Park–Kenwood's first planned community, it received wide and favorable publicity. And in 1885, Rosalie Music Hall on the southwest corner of 57th and Harper, designed by Beman, opened to become a center for social, musical, and political events.[77]

Pls. 27, 28

Pl. 29

Although Beman supervised all the houses and built several, other Chicago architects were also represented, both by the houses they built for clients and those they built for themselves as investment properties: among them were W. W. Boyington, H. F. Starbuck, and Irving Pond, who had been Beman's foreman. Many of these houses have been remodeled, but the one at 5736 Harper is unaltered.

A promotional brochure, "A Holiday at Rosalie Villas," published by James P. Craig, has pictures of the houses and the names of the people for whom they were built, as well as a few glimpses of interiors. The title of the brochure suggests that the houses may have been conceived originally as summer homes. If so they provide another example of the urban-rural paradox exemplified in John Dunham's property in Kenwood. For as soon as these houses were completed, South Park's first apartment building went up as a part of the same development. Its bay windows, designed to admit as much midwestern winter light as possible, were to become a feature of most apartment buildings in the area. Although in appearance it very much resembled a series of row houses, and its south front on Sylvia Court lent it a feeling of neighborly intimacy, it nevertheless represented a radical departure from the single-family home and heralded the beginning of increasing density in South Park.

Pl. 30

Blackstone Avenue, one block to the west, is dotted with modest frame houses; two, in the shingle style, are by W. Carbys Zimmerman, of the architectural firm of Flanders and Zimmerman. One was built for his own use, one as rental property.

Pl. 31

Pl. 32

By 1889 most of Dorchester Avenue between 57th and 59th streets had been developed by Claudius B. Nelson and his son Walter, a building contractor. The flat-roofed town houses on the west side of the street, built before 1882, reflect Nelson's belief in the future of the community and its inevitable urbanization. Across the street, the semidetached brick Queen Anne houses show the Nelsons keeping up with the changes in style, but still getting good use from the land.

Kenwood Avenue and Kimbark Avenue both have rows of freestanding frame pattern-book

Pl. 33

houses, some more elaborate than others. In general these houses are smaller than their Kenwood counterparts and are set on narrower lots with shallower yards. Unlike the Kenwood houses, which used a variety of materials—wood, brick, stone, stucco—these tend to be built entirely of wood, the ornamentation coming from the porch spindles and the use of fish-scale shingles.

Beyond Kimbark, except for the Shorey house, the Home for Incurables on Ellis, and a few cottages on Drexel, the land was vacant swamp.

In 1889, the seeds of urbanization were all there: strong physical and economic ties with the city, a varied population, a sophisticated intellectual and cultural life, and a wide supply of housing that included fashionable mansions, comfortable middle-class homes, and houses for workingmen. There were one active commercial center and two local shopping areas. And there was still plenty of undeveloped land; much of it had been subdivided, in anticipation of development, for several decades.

By the time Hyde Park–Kenwood joined Chicago it was reproducing, on a smaller scale, the city's own pattern of growth: a closely populated commercial center, with residential rings (or half-circles, the lake forming the eastern boundary) decreasing in density as they moved outwards. The population of Hyde Park Center, the first area of settlement, had grown to more than 20,000.[78] It was no longer so desirable to live close to the tracks; trains were larger, noisier, dirtier, and more frequent than they had been in 1856. During the next decade the frame houses and large yards of the first families who settled on Cornell Avenue near the station—the Jamesons, the Hopkinses, the Mulveys—would be replaced by row houses and three-story apartment buildings. Just west of the tracks Lake Park Avenue, precisely because it was close to the station, was becoming the place where the least attractive businesses were located: the liquor stores, coal yards, wagon- and harnessmakers, blacksmiths, and livery stables. Big houses on Lake Park Avenue, built for Chicago's elite, were being converted into boarding houses for men who worked on the trains or in the hotel. And some people were again following the pattern they had followed in leaving Chicago. J. N. Barker left the house toward which Lake Park Avenue was stretching its long commercial finger and built a new one at 50th and Greenwood; R. R. Donnelley, founder of the printing firm, who had moved to Hyde Park Center in the seventies, built a house at 46th and Woodlawn; B. F. Ulrich, one of Hyde Park's earliest real estate men, moved from 51st Street to Kenwood. In another manner, presaging future urban behavior, Paul Cornell chose to go "in" rather than "out." He built and moved into the new seven-story Hyde Park Hotel. It was a residential hotel that in elegance and exclusiveness recalled the early suburban visions.

3   A City Neighborhood
1890–1910

During the twenty years following annexation, Hyde Park–Kenwood burst out of its chrysalis into a colorful and highly variegated being. It attracted people with brains, money, and talent. There was a massive influx from Chicago proper, stimulated by the activities of builders and developers. Many of the newcomers employed the best Chicago architects, both traditional and innovative, to design their homes. The apartments and houses from this period reflect most of the important design trends in the Midwest.

The twin catalysts of change were the 1893 world's fair and the new University of Chicago. Neither would have come to the neighborhood had it not become part of the city.

The World's Columbian Exposition of 1893

Fig. 11

Less than a year after Hyde Park–Kenwood joined Chicago, Congress passed an act creating the World's Columbian Exposition in celebration of the four hundredth anniversary of the discovery of America. The act, signed by President Harrison, called for an "international exhibition of arts, industries, manufactures, and products of the soil, mine, and sea" and provided for commissioners representing all the states and territories; there was also a parallel "Board of Lady Managers."

Enterprising Chicagoans successfully promoted their city as the site, aided, as they had anticipated, by the fact that it was now the second largest in the United States. Several arguments were put forth for the Chicago location: it was central, with thirty railroads terminating in the city; its phenomenal growth and great advances typified New World development; it would be better to bring foreign visitors deep into America than to let them see only New York; and it would be easier to find a suitable site in Chicago.

Initially a downtown location was considered, on the lakefront between Michigan Avenue and the Illinois Central tracks, and beyond the tracks on land to be formed by fill. But downtown businessmen objected, both because of the expense of the fill and the effect the

45

46

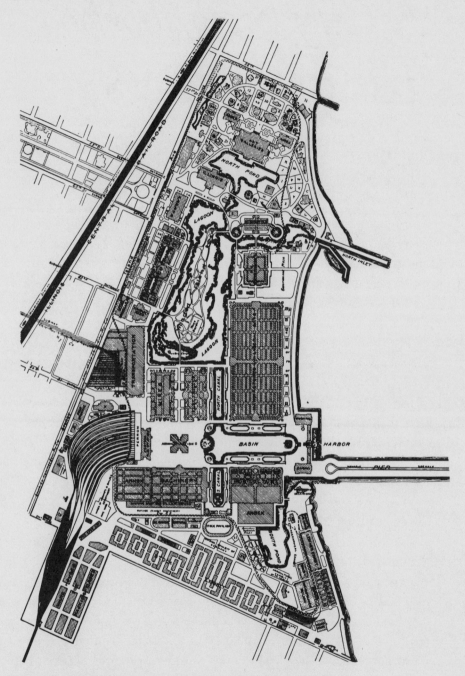

Fig. 11. The World's Columbian Exposition, 1893. (From
the official *Book of the Fair*, 1895)

exposition would have on adjacent real estate values. The West Parks were reviewed and rejected because they were too far from the lake.

Daniel Burnham, chief architect for the exposition, favored Jackson Park. Only the north end had been improved at that time; the part on which most of the exposition would be built was mainly low and marshy, covered with water, dotted with scrub oaks. Frederick Law Olmsted, who had prepared a plan for the South Parks twenty years earlier, was invited to come out and evaluate the situation. He and the consulting architects determined on a plan that involved a system of navigable waterways very similar to the one he had proposed earlier. The South Park Board was persuaded to add to the unimproved land the already improved north part and the Midway Plaisance, making 650 acres in all.

On a bright June day, in 1890, Burnham brought the national commissioners to visit Jackson Park, taking a boat from the foot of Harrison Street, and returning downtown on the Illinois Central. They were favorably impressed with the location, and the city's choice was confirmed. Prominent men in Hyde Park–Kenwood became involved in the exposition plans: some were on the board of directors, including George M. Bogue; William K. Ackerman was auditor; Benjamin F. Ayer, Lyman Trumbull, James P. Root, and John A. Jameson, all old settlers, served on the lawyers committee.

The problem of furnishing transportation for fair visitors was a major one, and it was attacked promptly. The challenge was how to move at least three hundred thousand people—nearly one-third of the permanent population of Chicago—to and from the fairgrounds each day. (On Chicago Day it proved to be five hundred thousand people.) The Illinois Central raised its tracks from 53d to 67th streets, enlarged its Van Buren Street Station, bought forty-one new locomotives and three hundred new side-door cars. The elevated railway, originating at 12th Street, was extended to come in above the raised tracks of the Illinois Central at 63d Street, with its terminal on the roof of the Transportation Building annex.[1]

Figs. 12, 13, 14

Immediately, property values in the vicinity of Jackson Park went up, and there was great speculative activity around the site of the fair. But there was also some concern about its effect on the finer residential sections. The *Chicago Tribune* in May 1892 remarked that "these sections, under ordinary conditions, would have developed as high class residence districts exclusively. The location of the Fair, however, has stimulated the construction of apartment houses in neighborhoods where they are not actually needed and where they are not appreciated by surrounding owners."[2] By September *The Economist* (a weekly covering financial, commercial, and real estate news), was able to report that there was more building in Hyde Park than at any time in its history. At the same time, building costs were going up because of

48

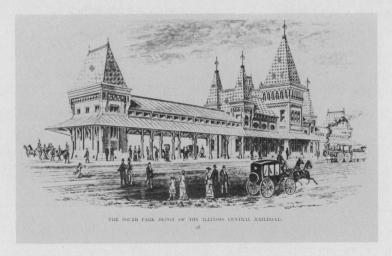

THE SOUTH PARK DEPOT OF THE ILLINOIS CENTRAL RAILROAD.

Fig. 12. Illinois Central station at 57th Street (South Park).
(Courtesy of the Illinois Central Gulf Railroad)

Fig. 13. Looking west on 57th Street, about 1890. The
apartment house at the left is still standing, but the stores
on the right went down during urban renewal. (Courtesy
of the Illinois Central Gulf Railroad)

Fig. 14. Illinois Central station at 57th Street (South Park) after the tracks had been elevated for the World's Columbian Exposition in 1893. (Courtesy of the Chicago Historical Society)

the unprecedented demand for men and materials created by the fair.[3] In October the *Tribune* stated that fully three million dollars was being expended on hotels and apartment buildings. They were constructed of brick and stone, as the fire limits had been extended to 67th Street, leaving only the district south of the park open for temporary residential structures.[4] In addition to the Hyde Park Hotel, already completed, three luxury hotels, the old Windermere, the Chicago Beach, at 51st Street and Hyde Park Boulevard, and the Del Prado, on 59th Street between Dorchester and Blackstone, were going up. (All are now demolished.) Some smaller hotels, apartment buildings, and boarding houses were being built, and stores with flats above them were beginning to line 55th Street. But the main building push was south of the Midway, in Woodlawn, for it was there that both the Illinois Central and the "El" trains would terminate; the main entrance to the fair was to be at 63d Street.

Community feelings about what was happening to the neighborhood, its property values, and its village atmosphere must have been mixed. We get intimations of how some people felt in *Sweet Clover,* a romance about the exposition written by a young woman who had grown up in Hyde Park, which "still bore the traces of a country village. The young people walked through fields of sweet clover and goldenrod where now massive hotels and blocks of granite and glass appear."[5] Later, the heroine remarks to an acquaintance, "I suppose the Eastern people think we enjoy the prospect of being jostled and crowded and having our streets torn up and our city extended, and all our comfort taken away for two years while we live in perfect Pandemonium. No, we do not enjoy it, but we do it as our duty because we know that we can and shall do it well."[6]

In the spring of 1891 a thousand men began to prepare Jackson Park for the fair, leveling, planting, digging lagoons. Three tent villages were set up in the park. Architects and sculptors camped there with the laborers. Daniel Burnham's partner, John Root, lived on the site, and so did Augustus St. Gaudens, the sculptor, who wrote nostalgically of the almost two years he lived in a cabin in Jackson Park, "Days I spent there linger in the memory like a glorious dream. It seems impossible that such a vision can ever be recalled in its poetic grandeur and elevation."[7] Lorado Taft came to supervise the sculpture workshops, and stayed on to become an important artist in the community.

From other cities the board of architects included George B. Post, R. M. Hunt, and McKim, Meade, and White of New York, Peabody and Stearns of Boston, Van Brunt and Howe of Kansas City. From Chicago, in addition to Burnham and Root, there were Adler and Sullivan, Solon S. Beman, W. L. B. Jenney, and Burling and Whitehouse.

Frederick Law Olmsted returned to Chicago to do the landscaping and planting. Writing for the *Inland Architect* in September 1893, he recalled that in preparation for the fair they planted 100,000 small willows on the shores of the lagoons; 75 large carloads of collected herbaceous aquatic plants taken from the wild; 140,000 other aquatic plants, largely native and Japanese irises; and 285,000 ferns and other perennial herbaceous plants. The Wooded Island was specially designed by Olmsted as a peaceful sylvan retreat from the hurly-burly of the fair and its crowds.[8]

In October 1892 Chicago celebrated Columbus's discovery of America and dedicated the palaces of the world's fair with a spectacular program of civic dinners, parades, martial and ethnic music, and fireworks. Dignitaries came from all over the world; Chicagoans, rich and poor, decorated homes, offices, and stores, and turned out to watch, march, and cheer. The colorful procession to the dedication started at the Auditorium on Michigan Avenue and ended in Jackson Park with a volcano of flame and smoke as the artillery thundered a welcome.

The day was celebrated with invocations, speeches, and a lengthy ode by poet Harriet Monroe—all heard but dimly by the milling throngs. That night in every park in Chicago great fireworks displays closed the exciting day.[9]

Although the dedication took place in October, the exposition itself did not open until the following spring. All during the long cold winter thousands of workmen toiled in the sleet and snow to complete the buildings and landscaping.

The opening was every bit as spectacular as the dedication. It is described in *Sweet Clover*. After President Cleveland pressed the electric button that opened the fair, "down fell the veil from the golden Republic, up streamed the enormous jets of water from the fountains; color and movement thrilled along the roofs of the snowy palaces; flags of all nations unfurled gayly from myriad staffs; the boom of artillery thundered from the lake side; and as the multitude, swayed by mighty feeling, rent the air with cheers, the sun burst from a cloud and blessed the scene with a new splendor."[10] The local people must have felt well rewarded for their sacrifices and inconveniences.

It was a wonderful summer for those who lived within walking or commuting distance of the fair. Families entertained friends and relatives from all over the country. Described always as a dream city of unsurpassed beauty, the exposition offered an incredible amount of amusement and instruction: boat rides along the lagoons; exhibits ranging from buttons to boilers and constituting a true encyclopedia of the raw and wrought goods of the whole world. A rich array of special events, conferences, lectures, concerts, theatrical performances, ethnic celebrations, was spread over the summer. Special days honored states and nations. People came by the thousands to marvel and they were not disappointed.

The Midway was lined with encampments of exotic people: Indians both American and Asian, Arabs, Bedouins, Samoans, Egyptians, and Eskimos (who suffered visibly through the sweltering Chicago summer). Hundreds of concessions sold American and foreign food and drink. And over all towered the giant Ferris wheel, 264 feet high, slowly revolving so that all its riders could view the full splendor of the exposition set in the lagoons.

Then suddenly, by fall, it was over. Although the main fair buildings remained open to visitors through most of November, the attractions on the Midway Plaisance were closed. As one student wrote glumly in the *University of Chicago Weekly*, "No more shall we gaze from our dormitory windows upon the gay throng of Europeans and Asiatics, Mongolians, Caucasians, Ethiopians, Columbia guards and World's Fair directors."[11]

The buildings, the sculpture, the fountains, had all been made of "staff," a material composed of plaster of Paris and hemp, which could be shaped in molds. From the beginning

Fig. 15

Fig. 15. The Ferris Wheel on the Midway. Foster Hall,
one of the university's new women's dormitories, appears
at the left. (Courtesy of the University of Chicago Library,
Department of Special Collections)

they had been intended to be temporary. But evidently in the excitement of planning and the
press of construction no one had contemplated the question of what to do with this great
production when the fair was over.

The problem was solved, intentionally or by accident, on the night of January 8, 1894,
when masses of silent onlookers watched the whole fantastic creation burn. Again, our student
reports, "I stood on the Plaza in the Court of Honor last night and watched the 'Dream City'
disappear in flames. The whole East was illuminated by this Funeral Pyre of Beauty, a mass of

moving luminous light, mounting higher and higher against the blue black sky, with great flames changing from gold into deepest crimson."[12]

A few structures were spared. The Fine Arts Building, designed by Charles Atwood of Burnham and Root, remained. It had been constructed of brick under the staff, to safeguard its precious contents. Marshall Field gave a million dollars so that it could be converted into a museum housing collections acquired from world's fair exhibitors. Many years later, when the Field Museum got its new building downtown, Julius Rosenwald, a Kenwood resident, made possible the renovation of the Fine Arts Building and its conversion into the Museum of Science and Industry. A group of South Shore women persuaded the Spanish Consulate to allow them to use La Rábida, the replica of the monastery where Columbus stayed while awaiting Queen Isabella's permission to make his voyage, for a children's hospital. The original building survived until 1918. The German Building nearby was spared until it burned in 1925, and the arcaded stone Iowa Building near the present Promontory survived for many years, used as a park shelter. The Japanese tea houses, still smelling sweetly of oriental woods, continued to grace the Wooded Island until well into the thirties. And on 57th Street a row of frame concession buildings, designed by George Beaumont,[13] survived until the sixties, when they succumbed to urban renewal. After 1912 these became a center for artists, writers, and philosophers. And for many years the replicas of the ships that brought Columbus to America, the Niña, the Pinta, and the Santa Maria, floated in the Jackson Park Lagoon, making it a place of history and romance for the children of the neighborhood. The *Statue of the Republic,* affectionately known as "the Golden Lady," in Jackson Park at 65th Street, is a replica, about half the size of the original by Daniel Chester French.

Fig. 16

Fig. 17

The 650 acres remained a barren waste until 1901, when the city moved topsoil from one of the richest farms in Will County into the park at a rate of twenty-five carloads, or nine hundred cubic yards, a day, in an effort to revitalize the area.[14]

Even as the fair lay in ruins it was apparent that it had been more than a dream city, more than a museum, more than a playground. In its all-embracing vastness it had gathered up and presented to millions of people much that was new and challenging in every field of human activity. It was described in the guidebooks as the marvel of the century, a comprehensive picture of civilization, the culmination of all the progress made by the nations of the earth in the centuries that had passed, and the gathering together of all that science, art, and ingenuity had produced for the benefit of mankind.

Its effects were international, national, and local. The World's Congress Auxiliary, the intellectual and moral branch of the exposition, brought people together from all over the

Fig. 16. Japanese tea houses on the Wooded Island in
Jackson Park. (Courtesy of the Chicago Historical Society)

Fig. 17. Replicas of Columbus's ships in the Jackson Park
lagoon. (Courtesy of the University of Chicago Library,
Department of Special Collections)

world to present papers and hold discussions on literature, government, music, education, science, art, engineering, and religion, establishing permanent ties between nations and opening the eyes of many to new ways of thinking about God, man, and the world.

For women in particular the fair marked a turning point in their struggle for recognition and an opportunity to develop their organizational skills. The Board of Lady Managers strove to present "a complete picture of the women in every country of the world . . . and more particularly of those who are bread-winners." They wanted to find out whether women continued to do "the hard, wearing work of the world at prices which will not maintain life, and under unhealthy conditions; whether they have access to the common schools and colleges, and after having taken the prescribed course are permitted graduating honors; whether the women, in countries where educational facilities are afforded them, take a higher stand in all the active industries of life as well as in intellectual pursuits."[15] Headed by Bertha Honoré Palmer, the Board of Lady Managers enrolled foreign women and created the most powerful women's organization that had ever existed. There were official committees in England France, Italy, Germany, Spain, Austria, Russia, Belgium, Holland, Sweden, Norway, Greece, Siam, Japan, Algeria, Cape Colony, Cuba, Mexico, Nicaragua, Argentina, Jamaica, Ceylon, Brazil, Colombia, Ecuador, Venezuela, Panama, and the Sandwich Islands.[16]

The Woman's Building was designed by a woman architect, Sophia Hayden, an 1890 graduate of the Massachusetts Institute of Technology. In it arts and crafts from every nation were shown, concerts held, lectures and symposia on women in science, literature, education, and industry offered. Women's associations and their purposes were discussed, as were the rights of women in various countries. And, true to their more traditional conceptions of their role, the women provided and operated the Children's Building with its educational materials and the Department of Public Comfort which supplied a day-care center.

The experiences of working with groups and the contacts they made, both national and international, prepared women for the active role they would play in movements of political and social reform. At the same time, the technology exhibited at the fair was beginning to release them from their housekeeping chores and suggesting that homes, like factories, could and should be scientifically managed. This was echoed in Marion Talbot's efforts at the University of Chicago to systematize and rationalize women's lives, bringing the findings of science to the arts of family raising and housekeeping.

Of particular interest was the "electric house." In it the doorbell was rung from a pushbutton; the lights in the hall and all the rooms were controlled from a central panel as well as from the door of each room. An electric burglar alarm protected the family, and the apartments were warmed by electric radiators and cooled by electric fans. Food was cooked on an electric range and lowered to the dining room on an electric dumbwaiter. Dishes were washed by an electric dishwasher. And the house was equipped with a telephone, writing telegraph instrument, phonograph, and electric music box.[17]

Exhibits of building materials and home furnishings set new trends. One section of the Manufactures Building displayed bricks of all kinds, shapes, and sizes, showing their uses in walls, arches, gateways, chimney pieces, window openings, and cornices.[18] Other exhibits demonstrated the uses of ceramic tiles, the latest developments and most beautiful designs in bathtubs, toilets, wash basins, radiators, furnaces, and fireplaces.

Seeing the architecture of other lands, particularly the Japanese buildings, stimulated new thinking about design. The very architecture of the fair itself, the white neoclassical buildings, provided a model for public buildings in America for decades to come, an influence deplored by Louis Sullivan as destructive of the true creativity that had begun to stir American architecture.

At least as far-reaching as the influence on architectural styles, and in the end more enduring, was the basic idea embodied in the exposition, that a city could be planned, that a reasoned approach to the problems of site use, transportation, sanitation, lighting, and recreation was possible. The city plan was born with the exposition and came to maturity in subsequent years in Daniel Burnham's work in Chicago and other cities, both in the United States and abroad.

Locally, the fair's effect was threefold. The special transportation facilities that had been created enabled people to move faster and more easily into and out of the Hyde Park–Kenwood area, multiplying contacts with other parts of Chicago and opening up the neighborhood to new residents from other sections of the city. Second, the apartments and hotels that had been built formed a large housing stock for newcomers. Third, the huge crowds that the fair drew not only threatened the villagelike atmosphere but precipitated fresh controversy about the liquor laws.[19]

Fig. 18

A good deal of effort and emotion had been expended in keeping Hyde Park–Kenwood, with the exception of Lake Park Avenue, dry over the years, and as the fair opened the citizens, through the newly formed Hyde Park Protective Association, fought to maintain the Sunday closing laws, but without success. In the end these laws were waived on two grounds: it would be unfair to deprive the working classes of the joys of the fair, to which many of them could come only on Sunday, and the city wouldn't be able to handle the hordes of idle visitors were the fair to be closed that day.[20] Unarticulated, but no doubt a factor, was the loss of revenue were the fair to be closed on Sundays.

Although they lost the fight over Sunday closing, members of the Hyde Park Protective

Fig. 18. Liquor store on the northeast corner of 55th
and Lake Park, 1892. Note the wooden sidewalks and cable
car tracks. (Courtesy of the Illinois Central Gulf Railroad)

Association went forth to do battle with the hotels that had been built for the exposition and
the liquor interests that wanted an entering wedge near Jackson Park. They badgered the hotel
keepers, many of whom claimed they were losing money anyway, trying to get them to stop
serving wine and beer. The hotel keepers protested that foreign visitors expected wine and
beer with their meals. A compromise of sorts was reached, and many of the hotel keepers
agreed not to have bars and to serve liquor only in residents' rooms or with meals. An
application for a liquor license in the dry area near the 57th Street station was successfully
fought, as were numerous other encroachments on the liquor laws over the next twenty years.
With the moral and financial assistance of the neighborhood church groups the Hyde Park
Protective Association moved relentlessly against blind pigs, sales of liquor in drugstores,
gambling, saloons, and beer gardens.

Hyde Park–Kenwood managed to hold the line through the efforts of the Hyde Park
Protective Association, but south of the Midway, saloons proliferated on 63d Street during

and after the fair. Drinking in the parks, particularly Washington Park, created a constant problem.[21]

Ethnic origins, class distinctions, and economic pressures all played a part in the motivation of the Hyde Park Protection Association. Those who drank in public places, in parks and saloons, were, by and large, immigrant laborers: Germans, Irish, Czechs, Italians, and Poles. Native Americans, people who had arrived financially, could drink in their clubs and could afford houses with large enough living rooms and dining rooms so they could entertain each other in their homes. Alcoholism was indeed a problem among the poor and underprivileged, and the Hyde Park Protective Association professed to be trying to save the workingman from his own vices. Although the organization was consistent in its attempt to maintain prohibition—trying, for instance, to put pressure on South Shore Country Club when it opened—the underlying fear that drove so many Hyde Parkers to participate in the association's crusade was that the big liquor interests would make a breakthrough in the neighborhood, opening it to a massive influx of foreignborn laborers and threatening property values.

The University of Chicago

The new University of Chicago opened a fortnight before the dedication of the exposition. Its students rejoiced in the pomp and glory of the parade that went down the Midway past their dormitory windows and eagerly anticipated the new knowledge and experience this fortunate juxtaposition would bring.

At the same time that plans were being made for the exposition, the efforts of Thomas Goodspeed, William Rainey Harper, and Frederick Gates to induce John D. Rockefeller to start a Baptist educational institution in Chicago had begun to bear fruit.

In May of 1889 the annual meeting of the American Baptist Education Society committed itself to founding a well-equipped college in Chicago. In fact, one of the resolutions stated specifically that the college must be in a city and not in a suburban village.[22]

The location had been the subject of lengthy discussion and correspondence. Thomas Goodspeed, in a letter to Rockefeller on January 7, 1887, argued for establishing the prospective Baptist university in Chicago on the grounds that the Baptists had no first-rate college in the West, that if they didn't educate their intelligent members they would lose them; they needed to raise an educated ministry, and Chicago as the commercial, political, social, religious, and educational center of a wide empire, was the natural place for everyone in the West to come to.[23]

Although Rockefeller at first wanted to endow a college, there were those in the American

Baptist Education Society who were pressing for a university. And for a university a city location was essential, as Augustus H. Strong pointed out in his 1889 plea for placing the institution in New York: the church should not let university education drift into the hands of skeptics, and the Baptists had no university with courses for all the professions. The city and the city only was the place for university work. Colleges and academies might be in smaller towns, but for men who were studying for professions the city with its "conditions of highest mental activity and growth," its close contacts and frequent meetings, its good communications by rail and press, made gaining and spreading new ideas easier and more rapid.[24]

To the suggestion that Morgan Park, a suburb to the south, was the logical place, Strong wrote to Rockefeller on February 17, 1887, that it was too far away. "Every theological seminary ought to be in the midst of the thickest of life."[25] Frederick Gates, too, thought Morgan Park too remote, and in a paper delivered to the Baptist Ministers' Conference in October 1888 he deplored the Baptists' "present policy of locating feeble institutions in obscure towns."[26]

Two other arguments put forth by Gates, October 23, 1888, may have clinched the matter: "If some Christian denomination does not go in and capture the city, infidelity will"; furthermore, it should be easier to raise money from non-Baptists if the institution were located within the city.[27] George Northrup agreed, and in a letter to Dr. Harper on December 6, 1888, he added that students of religion who studied in the city would be brought into more vital relations with city churches, prayer meetings, public services, and missions.[28] The Baptists needed a city, and Chicago needed a university, the first one having been forced to close because of financial difficulties.

Rockefeller agreed to put up six hundred thousand dollars if the American Baptist Education Society would guarantee to raise another million, and when his offer was announced at the society's meeting it was greeted with tumultuous cheering and applause. Though not yet a university the new college was founded with expectations of greatness, and it was incorporated under the old title, the University of Chicago.[29]

By January of 1890 one of Chicago's outstanding merchants, Marshall Field, had promised to give the university its first ten acres and to sell it ten more[30]—in all, twenty acres of sand and swamp, laced with barbed wire fences—land that he had been holding since 1879.[31]

Frederick Gates wrote to H. L. Morehouse on January 17 describing the location of the prospective university.

I wrote you a card announcing Mr. Field's gift. It is located twenty-one blocks south and four blocks east of the old site. The land is sufficiently elevated and drained—an important item here—is one block from the Cottage Grove Avenue grip line running down this Ave.

and Wabash to heart of city, the loop turning on Lake Street. From the river dividing the north and south sides, it is a 45 minutes ride in "grip" to the site. The Ill. Cent. line with its city and suburban trains runs about 8 or 10 minutes walk from campus, with depot on nearest point of line. From this depot to Ill. Cent. (and Mich. Cent) depot the time is 25 minutes, 47 trains running each way daily. It takes about same time to reach campus from the river between north and south sides by Ill. Cent. R.R. as to reach N.Y. Cent. Depot on 42nd St. from Post Office in New York by elevated road. Besides these means of access there are two lines of street railway running east and west across the city just below the campus. These lines tap the whole southwest section of the city. The territory of the South Side and especially that for several miles in every direction from the site is residence property and forms the location of the higher middle and aristocratic classes. No manufacturing will ever be possible in the neighborhood. The land lies about 1200 feet east of Washington Park and about 2000 feet west of Jackson Park. These are the two great parks of the South Side and are being developed with vast expense into great beauty. Each contains several hundred acres. The "Plaisance" which connects these two parks with a waterway Boulevard and pleasure grounds runs two blocks south of the site.[32]

By June 1891 Henry Ives Cobb had been selected as the architect who, working from sketches and plans proposed by Martin Ryerson and Charles Hutchinson, would design a campus in the neo-Gothic style.

At last Paul Cornell's dream was to be fulfilled. He had chosen the site, initiated the transportation, planned the parks, excluded industry, encouraged "higher middle and aristocratic classes," and now there was to be the long-hoped-for institution. The university was to be, in effect, a nonpolluting industry, with enormous investments of funds, a great staff of agents, officers, and employees, and what President Harper would later call a "hotel system," requiring housekeepers, janitors, cooks, servants, and watchmen. For the first time Hyde Park–Kenwood would be exporting services beyond its own boundaries and bringing in workers for its institution.

The University and the Community: The Reform Movement

The Baptists chose a city location because they wanted to take part in city life. The new university was not to be an ivory tower, but was to be profoundly involved in solving man's problems. The opportunity for this kind of activity presented itself almost immediately.

As the fair opened in the spring there were indications that the economy of the country was in trouble. The stock market had sagged, and though the eager crowds in Chicago were seemingly unaware of, or purposely ignoring, the situation, the country was slipping into a deep depression. The full effects began to be felt in Chicago as the closing of the fair left in its wake thousands of homeless and unemployed.

Robert Morss Lovett, in his autobiography, recalls the appalling contrast between the artificial glory of the fair and the squalor of the real city. The aftermath of the fair could be seen in blocks of vacant houses and boarded-up hotels. And from their dormitory windows the same students who had watched the opulent procession to the fair and the colorful life on the Midway now saw Coxey's Army of Unemployed straggle north to seek food and shelter in the city.[33]

There had been warnings that all was not as ideal as the city of gilt and plaster might have led one to think. The rift between labor and capital had been growing steadily since the first strikes in the seventies. The scars of the McCormick Reaper strike, followed by the Haymarket debacle, were still fresh. Unionism, socialism, anarchism, were very much on people's minds. The Hyde Park Philosophical Society discussed them all, together and in sequence. The steady influx of poor, unskilled, bewildered immigrants living in flimsy and unsanitary housing had aroused the concern of a few people, among them Jane Addams, who had established Hull House in 1889.

Chicago had always had the reputation of being a wide-open town where drinking, gambling, and prostitution flourished. Mayor John Roche's attempts to clean up the city came to an abrupt end with the election of Carter Harrison, Sr., who virtually assured the leaders of the vice rings that at least for the summer of the fair it would be business as usual.

Among many prosperous Chicagoans, in addition to the anxiety aroused by labor unrest and concern about poverty and vice, there had always been a feeling of self-consciousness about the city's materialism, the emphasis on getting rich. Although from the very first there had been people living in Hyde Park–Kenwood who worked to bring "culture" to the city—the Scammonses, Roots, Hitchcocks, and Ryersons, among others—the myth prevailed that despite evidence to the contrary, the industrialists of Porkopolis were universally crass, money-grubbing, bent only on self-aggrandizement.

With the end of the fair, the onslaught of the depression, and the opening of the new university, came a period of reform that reached into every section of urban life and involved some of Chicago's wealthiest and most powerful men. People in Hyde Park–Kenwood, now inextricably a part of the city, were very active in the movement. The university saw itself as having a Christian mission, and its Department of Sociology, the first in the country, envisioned its role as one of Christian reform.

William Stead, an Englishman who had come to report on the fair for his newspaper, sparked the reform movement. Appalled at what he found in the city, he produced a book, *If Christ Came to Chicago,* which described in lurid detail the prostitution, gambling, corruption, and poverty. The book's candor scandalized and terrified Chicagoans who were still congratulating themselves on the splendid image their fair had earned for them. Mothers hid the book from their children, but the truth of its allegations could not be denied.

On November 12, 1893, William Stead, under labor union auspices, called a mass meeting of concerned Chicagoans. According to Graham Taylor's description, sitting side by side were leading businessmen and labor leaders, representatives of the city government and of its exclusive clubs, preachers and saloonkeepers, gamblers and theology professors, matrons of distinguished families and madams of brothels, judges of the courts and one of the men convicted in the Haymarket riot trials.

Although there seemingly had been no plan of action before the meeting, a program emerged for a federation for the relief of the poor, industrial reconciliation, war against slums and vicious elements of society, and the improvement of the quality of municipal government. Lyman Gage was elected president, and Mrs. Potter Palmer, who had served so admirably as president of the Board of Lady Managers of the fair, was made first vice-president of the new Civic Federation. Prominent on the first board was Albion Small, chairman of the university's Department of Sociology, whose interest in social dynamics propelled him into participating in municipal affairs. Professor Edward Bemis, of the university's Department of Education, was also involved, as were, eventually, many members of the Hyde Park–Kenwood community, including such prominent businessmen as Bernard E. Sunny and Julius Rosenwald.

An immense organization sprang from these early efforts: thirty-four councils sent representatives to its central committee. Thomas E. Donnelley, son of Richard Robert Donnelley, helped organize the Hyde Park Council of the Civic Federation in 1894. During subsequent years community members participated in each of the federation's six departments: Philanthropical, Political, Industrial, Educational, Moral, and Municipal.[34]

The momentum of the reform movement carried it well into the first decade of the twentieth century, and University of Chicago professors continued to take an active part. In 1905 the City Club asked Professor Charles E. Merriam to do a study of the city's municipal revenues, the findings of which were published in a series in the *Chicago Tribune.*[35] Merriam also studied the city's water and shipping facilities. Stimulated to involve himself in municipal politics, he ran successfully for alderman in 1909. In this position he introduced an ordinance for a commission to investigate city expenditures, and when it was organized the mayor appointed him head of it. Perhaps predictably, the picture of graft and corruption that the Merriam Commission uncovered was so embarrassing to the city that the commission's funds were cut off.[36]

Through the Civic Federation and its related activities contacts between the business and intellectual communities were frequent. Although in the nineties and early 1900s there was a trend toward separation of the two groups—the university families living south of 55th Street, the wealthy brokers, bankers, and industrialists north of 51st—the division was not absolute; the lines blurred as businessmen, doctors, and lawyers moved their families into the university neighborhood, and men and women from both sections worked together on civic problems.

The business community had rallied generously in the university's opening fund-raising efforts, and both groups were eager to use each other fruitfully. When the Civic Federation held a conference on trusts, President Harper and W. B. Conkey, president of the Illinois Manufacturers' Association, served together on the committee on arrangements. And when the Civic Federation chose to investigate the public school system, President Harper headed a Committee of One Hundred recommending revisions of Chicago school law. In 1907 Ernst Freund of the University of Chicago Law School drafted the city charter on revenue and taxation for the Illinois legislators. Town and gown were united in their work for a better Chicago.[37]

Equally active in the network of reform organizations was the Chicago Woman's Club. Its ambitious and far-reaching program drew many women from the Hyde Park–Kenwood community. The club's yearbook for 1892–93 listed about forty active members from the area, among them Mrs. J. Frank Aldrich, Mrs. Henry Varnum Freeman (wife of the judge and former village attorney), Mrs. Leslie Lewis (wife of the superintendent of schools), Mrs. John Nolan, Mrs. Martin Ryerson, Mrs. Daniel Shorey, Mrs. A. G. Spaulding, Mrs. Helen Starrett, Mrs. Joseph Twyman, Mrs. Fannie Bloomfield Zeisler, and Mrs. Pennoyer Sherman.

During this year President Harper spoke to them on "The Relation of Women to the University" and asked their help in raising money for women's dormitories. A committee was created, and by the following fall $170,000 had been raised, enough money to build Foster, Kelly, and Beecher Halls, and make a start on Green.[38]

Over the next two decades the Woman's Club worked diligently, often in cooperation with other organizations, frequently with the guidance and assistance of University of Chicago faculty, on problems of municipal government, public schools, crime and law enforcement, public health, and public welfare. In all these activities women of Hyde Park–Kenwood consistently took positions of leadership.

Serving on committees, working with the university, lecturing, prodding, publicizing, in both the Civic Federation and the Chicago Woman's Club, were those two redoubtable women, Jane Addams and Mary McDowell, heads of Hull House and the University of Chicago Settlement, respectively. The University of Chicago Settlement, modeled on Hull House, was founded, shortly after the university opened, in rooms above a feed store back of the stockyards. Students and faculty contributed time and money to programs designed to educate workers and their families and to better their living conditions. Jane Addams and Mary McDowell were the consciences of the city, working tirelessly for the poor and the deprived, combining philanthropy with a hard-headed and sophisticated approach to munici-pal problems and legislative reform.

The ardor of the reformers was fanned by two major events, occurring within a few years of each other, intensely experienced both locally and nationally: the Pullman strike in 1894, and, in 1901, the assassination of President McKinley by a self-avowed anarchist.

Although the Central Relief Association, organized by the Civic Federation, did much to help the hungry and homeless during the first desperate winter after the fair, its work could be only palliative; it could not alter the grim fact of the depression with its pay cuts and layoffs. An outgrowth of the depression, the Pullman strike affected many members of the Hyde Park–Kenwood community. Only five years earlier, the community of Pullman, a few miles south on the Illinois Central line had shared a village government with Hyde Park–Kenwood. Contacts had been social as well as political. The theater George Pullman had given his town attracted trainloads of people from Hyde Park–Kenwood. And Pullmanites had attended social affairs in Flood Hall and Lynch's Hall. Pullman had been built as a model town from which all that was "ugly, discordant, and demoralizing" was eliminated. George Pullman thought of himself as a benevolent idealist as well as an industrialist. It probably never occurred to him that his men could be anything but grateful to him for embodying in himself that trinity of roles: employer, landlord, and moral dictator. He was, however, no sentimen-talist so far as his business was concerned, and in the spring of 1894, when the shop workmen protested the reductions in wages and the layoffs of workmen without a corresponding lowering of rents, George Pullman was unyielding. In May the Pullman car workers went on strike. They were still on strike when the newly organized American Railway Union, led by Eugene V. Debs, met in Chicago in June. After attempts to arbitrate with the Pullman Company failed, the union passed a boycott motion; Debs sent out two hundred telegrams to his members on western railroads ordering a boycott of Pullman cars. The cars were to be cut out of the trains and run onto sidings. As managers reacted and discharged workmen, sympathetic trade unions quit work. Although Debs pleaded for no violence, violence was inevitable. The railroad managers, determined not to be overcome by the union, tried to run the trains themselves; the workers reacted by stoning the trains and pushing them over. Riots, shootings, and fires followed. No cattle came into the stockyards, and no dressed meat went out. There was a threat of a real food shortage. Mail trains were delayed.[39]

For those who lived in Hyde Park–Kenwood it was a time of anxiety and tension. Night after night they could see the skies lighted by burning cars. Many families associated with the packing business lived in Kenwood. Railroad officials lived in both Kenwood and South Park, and men who worked in the car works or on the trains lived in Hyde Park Center. The Illinois Central trains that bore residents downtown to work carried riflemen seated in the engine cabs, and commuters sometimes had to flatten themselves on the train floor to avoid snipers' bullets.[40]

Fig. 19

President Cleveland, seeing a threat to the nation's food supply as well as to its stability, sent federal troops to camp in Grant Park. The general strike that Debs had tried to arrange with the American Federation of Labor never took place, and in time operations resumed at Pullman. But the violence that had erupted in the city during those hot summer months divided people into two groups, those who thought that the strikers were the embodiment of evil, and those who were horrified by the Pullman Company's persistent refusal to arbitrate and by the realization that its former employees were approaching starvation. Witness to the fears that were engendered are a few houses in Kenwood that were built with a third-floor section where the family could be sealed off and protected by metal doors.

Latent feelings were reactivated on September 7, 1901, when an assassin shot President McKinley as he attended the Pan-American Exposition in Buffalo. The assassin claimed to be an anarchist and asserted that he had only done his duty; valid anarchists deplored the crime and denied any association with him. Nevertheless, Chicago police swept the city, imprisoning known and suspected anarchists, including Emma Goldman, who was visiting Chicago.[41]

The difference in attitude between those who were working in the settlements and those who feared the laboring class was exemplified by the Reverend Joseph A. Vance of the Hyde Park Presbyterian Church: "It tears us with conflicting emotions of rage and sorrow as we think of this awful deed.... The responsibility for the crime ... must be charged on those whose lectures and books made him an anarchist."[42] Was he referring to the University Extension courses given in the settlements? To Thorstein Veblen, who taught a course in socialism? Or, perhaps, to Jane Addams and Mary McDowell, who often alienated their wealthy contributors by their controversial identification with the workers?

The Reverend Mr. Vance must have been voicing a common reaction. Jane Addams, later recalling this period, described the horror everyone felt at the assassination, but went on to say, "It seemed to me then that in the millions of words uttered and written at that time, no one adequately urged that public-spirited citizens set themselves the task of patiently discover-

Fig. 19. Federal troops encamped on the Chicago lakefront
during the Pullman strike of 1894. (Courtesy of the Chicago
Historical Society)

ing how these sporadic acts of violence against government may be understood and averted.
We do not know whether they occur among the discouraged and unassimilated immigrants
who might be cared for in such a way as enormously to lessen the probability of these acts, or
whether they are the result of anarchistic teaching. By hastily concluding that the latter is the
sole explanation for them, we make no attempt to heal and cure the situation."[43]

Although there may have been unity in fighting vice and municipal corruption, the
solutions for poverty and the problems of labor were not so clear. The industrialism that had
been deified by the fair was also a demon: it threatened human values, impoverishing workers

and destroying individuality. Mass production by making automatons of men deprived them of their creativity.

Anti-Industrialism

Discontent with a materialistic society and a search for new human values were expressed in literature, education, and art. Robert Herrick, William Vaughn Moody, Robert Morss Lovett, I. K. Friedman, and Edgar Lee Masters were members of the local community and a part of that larger group of Chicago literati who came to be known as the Chicago Realists. They were novelists and poets who were passionately committed to social justice and deeply concerned with individual responsibility. In Hyde Park–Kenwood they lived side by side with the tycoons of business in whose force and power they found a new immorality.

Herrick, Moody, and Lovett had been friends at Harvard. They came west together, lured by the high salaries at the new university. The contrast between the mature, cultivated, puritanical atmosphere of Cambridge, and what these young men saw as the ruthless and stark business culture of Chicago drew the Harvard émigrés into the closest sort of fellowship. All under thirty years old, ardent and idealistic, they lived together, wrote together, and reminisced about the East.

Herrick taught English and wrote novels that outraged Chicagoans. In them he combined realism and social criticism, describing a special background, either in business or one of the professions, through which a personal problem emerged, expressed in terms of the individual versus society. His book *Memoirs of an American Citizen,* which appeared in 1905, was probably hardest for the local community to take. Written in the first person, it is the story of a penniless young man who comes to Chicago in the eighties and gradually, by a series of sharp and often dishonest practices, rises to fame and fortune as a packer. Finally, through the machinations of his business friends he becomes a United States senator, presumably with the assignment of furthering the interests of the meat-packing business. Climbing the ladder of success, he sheds, one by one, his human sympathies and instincts of fairness, rationalizing his behavior with falsely virtuous interpretations. There were enough packers erecting stately homes in Kenwood for us safely to assume that the book caused a scandal.

William Vaughn Moody was a romantic poet, impatient—as was Herrick—with the necessity of teaching. In his poem "The Brute" Moody expressed his feelings about the whole of modern culture, particularly its machines and factories. The Brute was a symbol of the nineteenth-century mechanical and business genius, at first meant to serve mankind, but eventually destroying it. The only hope for salvation lay in the idealism and fundamental goodness of men.[44]

Moody died very young, in 1910, after a brief marriage to Harriet Tilden Brainard, a remarkable woman in her own right. She was an inspired and inspiring teacher of English at Hyde Park High School, and at the same time a successful businesswoman. She originated and ran the Home Delicacies Association, whose major customers were Marshall Field's and fashionable society women. The income from this business enabled her to offer hospitality to poets, artists, and intellectuals in her home at 2790 Groveland (Ellis).[45]

Lovett was one of the group that met in the Groveland house. More teacher and scholar than either Herrick or Moody, he produced fewer literary works. Nevertheless, those that he did write were also concerned with the struggle for an ethical structure. His novel *Richard Gresham,* published in 1904, is the story of a highly moral young man who, in the process of making retribution for his father's misdeeds, discovers that he himself has become involved in fraud. Eventually Lovett took his family to become a part of the Hull House group, participating in that group's work on behalf of the immigrant workers.

Less well known but even more emotionally anti-big business was I. K. Friedman, who did his graduate work at the university in English and philosophy. He wrote bitter novels about the wickedness of industrialization, the terrible conditions under which men worked, and the perplexities of the educated idealist.

The Groveland group also included Edgar Lee Masters, although he had no attachment, except through friends, with the university. A poet and a liberal lawyer, he wrote against war and imperialism. His support of liberal causes led Clarence Darrow, the fiery defender of the poor and oppressed, to offer him a partnership in his firm. As with his marriage to Helen Jenkins, this partnership ended in hostility and dissolution, but for the first decade of the twentieth century the firm was occupied with defending working people and labor groups.

The broadest possible mission of the university was an important element in President Harper's educational philosophy. Sociology, theology, law, education, and political science were instruments for improving the human lot. Beyond this, Harper saw the university as having a larger obligation to bring education to the masses. The University Extension offered courses all over the city and to all classes of people. The education of young people, too, was scrutinized and recast.

The Dewey School, so named for philosopher John Dewey, was first housed at 5714 Kimbark. After a number of moves it got its own building under the name of the University of Chicago Laboratory School. It became known worldwide for its radical teaching methods, stressing individual development and the preparation of children for social living.

One of the strong emphases of the school, and of the Chicago Manual Training School, which later became part of the high school, was on hand work and hand crafts, reflecting the growth of the Arts and Crafts movement in Chicago. Like the social reformers and the literary Realists, those involved in the Arts and Crafts movement attacked the evils and depersonalization resulting from the rapid growth of industrialism. Settlements, artists, and architects were drawn to it. Chicago was one of the first cities in America to feel the influence of this movement, and a number of people from Hyde Park–Kenwood were in its forefront. The Chicago Arts and Crafts Society was organized in 1897; for several years it held annual exhibits at the Art Institute. *House Beautiful,* first published in the late nineties, was the movement's spokesman and promoter, spearheading its influence on home furnishings; Marion Talbot, dean of women at the university, was its domestic science editor.

The Arts and Crafts movement had originated in England with William Morris. In Chicago his apostle was Joseph Twyman, who lived on Dorchester Avenue and worked for the Tobey Furniture Company, a retail store, where he had a special William Morris room. Twyman had visited Merton Abbey, where Morris had his workshops devoted to the hand crafts: glassmaking, weaving, pottery, and printing. The movement was weighted with social as well as artistic significance; like the other reform movements of the period it stressed the importance and integrity of the creative individual in an increasingly mechanized society. Twyman describes Morris's art as "eminently sociological," an art meant to be "of the people, for the people, and by the people, . . . live, full of power, vigor, usefulness."[46]

In 1903 Twyman, Richard Green McDougall, and Oscar Lovell Triggs, an English professor at the university, founded the William Morris Society to promote artistic craftsmanship.[47] The Arts and Crafts movement and literature came together in the Blue Sky Press, founded by Thomas Wood Stevens and Alfred G. Langworthy, who did most of the typesetting and printing themselves. It was a home operation, located first at 54th and University and later at 47th and Kenwood. From 1899 to 1906 the young men who ran it printed both classics and new works in small editions, on fine paper, beautifully illustrated and illuminated in the Art Nouveau style.[48] In 1901, a studio called the University Guild, under the direction of George Schreiber, had workshops, reportedly the best equipped in the city, at 5001 Lake Park Avenue.[49] A few years later the South Park Workshop was formed, housing artisans and offering instruction in arts and crafts.[50]

Like the movement for social reform and the new education, the Arts and Crafts movement offered women an opportunity to enter if not the mainstream of production at least one of its most inviting tributaries. Women's traditional painting, sketching, and needlework activities were expanded, given a new moral and philosophical basis and broad social significance.

The Local Life

Fig. 20

Around the edges of these wide-ranging movements life in Hyde Park–Kenwood was pleasant, gay, secure, and sociable. Those who worked for civic and philanthropic causes did so with a profound belief in the perfectability of the human condition. The church groups were untiring in their efforts to raise money and improve religious education. To the original Presbyterian, Episcopal, and Catholic churches had been added those of the Baptists, Methodists, Swedish Lutherans, and Christian Scientists. Church activities were an important part of the social life, as were the various women's groups that sewed for foreign missions. The Kenwood Club, financially the most prosperous in Chicago,[51] continued to provide family recreation, tennis tournaments, and parties of all kinds. In 1901 Winston Churchill spoke there to a record crowd on his experiences in the Boer War.[52] The Quadrangle Club, built for the faculty of the University, burned and was rebuilt in 1897 by Charles Atwood, a member of Daniel Burnham's firm.[53] It was moved in the twenties to 58th Street, where it is now known as Ingleside Hall. The Lyceum was absorbed by the Chicago Public Library. Plans were set in motion for a new building for the Hyde Park YMCA, and a new high school (now the Ray School), designed by Flanders and Zimmerman, opened in 1894. Hyde Park High School was said to be the finest in the state.[54]

Citizens worked to maintain the special qualities of the community. The Hyde Park Protective League persisted in its efforts to keep the Hyde Park prohibition laws and curb gambling; in time it was instrumental in the demise of the Washington Park Race Track. The South Park Improvement Association, organized in 1901 by Mrs. Frank Johnson and Mrs. Joseph Twyman, provided a street-cleaning service—a man with a cart who swept up refuse and horse droppings.[55] Later the association's Landscape Architecture Committee obtained trees and shrubs for its members at wholesale prices and supervised their planting. The face of Hyde Park–Kenwood was changing: many of the willows and cottonwoods were dying of old age, and others were being removed to allow for laying sewers and paving streets.

The Hyde Park Betterment League was formed to improve conditions "mentally, morally, and spiritually," in the saloon district on Lake Park. In 1909 the league was instrumental in having a new flat building for blacks erected on Lake Park.[56]

Protection, improvement, betterment—the words imply that the community was less than perfect, and yet they also carry with them the implication that its citizens believed in their own power to affect the physical and moral conditions of life.

Although there was still a suburban feeling, which organizations such as the Protective League and the Improvement Association tried to preserve, Hyde Park–Kenwood had changed

Fig. 20. Tennis in Jackson Park, photographed some time after 1893. (Courtesy of the Chicago Historical Society)

drastically. Thanks to the fair and the university, both its population and its retail business had expanded. The transportation provided to bring people to the fair now put residents in easy touch with all parts of the city. The university imported and exported people and ideas. The neighborhood harbored growing numbers of families, rich, poor, and in between, people with the widest variety of opinions and abilities.

General Trends in Housing

Movement into Hyde Park–Kenwood was stimulated not only by the attractiveness and accessibility of the neighborhood and by the availability of large tracts of undeveloped land but also by the deterioration of areas to the north and west, where the intrusion of new immigrants, factories, warehouses, and vice pushed older immigrants and higher-income classes into areas of growth. In Chicago, neighborhoods wore out fast. No doubt the various

72

Fig. 21

civic protective and improvement groups were well aware of this phenomenon. Prairie Avenue, once the most fashionable of neighborhoods, began to go downhill in the nineties, partly because of the closeness of a vice area, partly because it was so near the Illinois Central, with the inevitable sootiness that came with coal-burning trains.[57] Although some people were moving to the North Side, following Potter Palmer's lead, it was still possible to buy large parcels of land in the western parts of Hyde Park–Kenwood for less than they would cost on the North Side, and to build free-standing houses with expansive lawns, even tennis courts.

By 1900 there was rapid transportation to every part of the city. The Illinois Central could deliver people to Chicago's Loop in twelve minutes and to industrial South Chicago equally swiftly. The Cottage Grove cable car line, electrified in the nineties, served the western edge of the community and the people who lived on 55th Street. The 47th Street car line provided access to and from the stockyards. Other parts of the West Side could be reached via the Elevated, which ran above 63d Street.

Except for the well-to-do, however, high land values, particularly in the area close to the fair, and pressure for housing both for university people and Chicago's constantly growing population, resulted in extensive development of row houses and apartments.[58]

Apartment buildings had long been considered an innovative and useful solution to Chicago's ever-present housing shortage. They were a natural outgrowth of the family hotels and boarding houses in which so many Chicagoans lived as the city was being built. And, of course, for the real estate investor or developer the apartment offered by far the best return for his money. For some time the terms "apartment" and "flat" were differentiated. An apartment house had all the amenities of a fine hotel: lobby, restaurant or cafe, small shops, liveried staff.[59] Flats were simpler structures, often frame, usually two-storied, but sometimes built above stores. Gradually this distinction in nomenclature disappeared.

The range of multifamily dwellings in Hyde Park–Kenwood was from block-long three-story buildings, financed by large investors, not necessarily Chicagoans, to unpretentious two-flats built and lived in by local tradesmen. Often the three- and six-flat buildings were put up by men who were themselves in one of the building trades: stonecutting, decorating, lumber, glass, or plumbing.

Many of these buildings were poorly designed and cheaply built. There was recurring discussion in architectural circles of the problems of apartment design: lot use, fireproofing, ventilation, planning for privacy.[60] The result was that while Hyde Park–Kenwood had its share of buildings quickly run up by contractors, there were also many that were carefully, even elegantly designed, light, spacious, and equipped with such desirable built-ins as buffets, bookshelves, consoles, mirrors, hat trees, linen and cedar closets, stoves, iceboxes, and

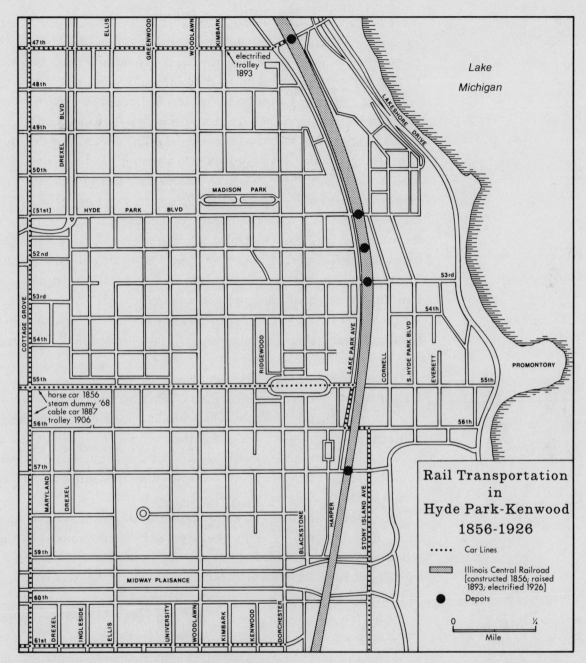

73

Fig. 21. Rail transportation in Hyde Park–Kenwood,
1856–1926.

(map labels)

Lake
Michigan

47th
48th
49th
50th
[51st]
52nd
53rd
54th
55th
56th
57th
59th
60th
61st

ELLIS
GREENWOOD
WOODLAWN
KIMBARK
BLVD
DREXEL
HYDE PARK BLVD
MADISON PARK
COTTAGE GROVE
RIDGEWOOD
LAKE PARK AVE
CORNELL
S. HYDE PARK BLVD
EVERETT
LAKE SHORE DRIVE
PROMONTORY
53rd
54th
55th
56th

MARYLAND
DREXEL
MIDWAY PLAISANCE
DREXEL
INGLESIDE
ELLIS
UNIVERSITY
WOODLAWN
KIMBARK
KENWOOD
DORCHESTER
BLACKSTONE
HARPER
STONY ISLAND AVE

electrified
trolley
1893

horse car 1856
steam dummy '68
cable car 1887
trolley 1906

Rail Transportation
in
Hyde Park-Kenwood
1856-1926

•••• Car Lines

▨ Illinois Central Railroad
[constructed 1856; raised
1893; electrified 1926]

● Depots

0   ¼
Mile

medicine cabinets. Certain architects came to specialize in apartment building: Andrew Sandegren, Thomas McCall, and the Doerr brothers. Others, who had become known for the houses they designed, the Ponds, the Rapps, Horatio Wilson, Ben Marshall, John Stone, and George Maher, designed apartment buildings as well.

During this period architectural style and interior furnishings were influenced by technological developments. The exhibits at the fair, noted earlier, put these before the public. The work of scientists also affected home design. The discovery of the microbe had a far-reaching influence on the way houses were built and furnished. Cleanliness assumed even greater importance than it had had before. Microbes lurked in heavily carved surfaces and deep-piled materials; sunshine and fresh air, as well as soap and water, were microbes' enemies. The use of the word "clean" to describe the lines of the new architecture and furniture was more than a metaphor. During the last decade of the nineteenth century and first decade of the twentieth, houses were opened up to air and light, and furniture was simplified. The brass or iron bed was more sanitary than a carved wooden bed; sleeping rooms and their furniture were painted white; kitchen walls were made of ceramic tile, as were bathrooms and vestibule floors. The velour draperies came off the windows, to be replaced by hand-blocked curtains. All at once the look of heavy ornamentation became unhealthful as well as unfashionable.[61]

The nineteenth-century anxieties aroused by rapid industrialization, social and economic inequities, and fear of disease had their parallel in fear of fire. Brick and stone replaced wood. The turreted, lavishly decorated Queen Anne houses of the eighties gave place to houses fashioned of brick, or brick and stone, their volumes simplified, their decoration derived from the use of the building materials. There was a new interest in American colonial houses; English domestic architecture slipped easily into the Gothic ambience of the university area, as well as the green stretches of Kenwood.

Interwoven in the fabric of social, educational, artistic, and architectural reform was a strong thread of morality. This morality was felt to be fostered by the home where spiritual and physical elements interacted to raise it to a higher level. Charles Henderson, professor of sociology in the Divinity School, and chaplain to the University, in his book *The Social Spirit in America,* considered homemaking fundamental to the virtuous life. "We make our houses and they turn upon us the image of our own taste and permanently fix it in our very nature. Our works and our surroundings corrupt or refine our souls. The dwelling, the walls, the windows, the roof, the furniture, the pictures, the ornaments, the dress, the fence or hedge—all act constantly upon the imagination and determine its contents. If a family realizes this truth, it will seek to beautify the objects which are silently and unceasingly writing their nature upon the man within the breast. When the families of a community give no heed to this truth there is missionary ground."[62]

Woman's responsibility in the creation of the home is stressed in the introduction to a book about American houses and social customs. "Education is rapidly becoming universal and with the acquirement of knowledge comes a development of taste and a new love for the beautiful. Woman has been emancipated and has taken an enviable place among the thinkers and doers of the world. But nowhere is her new power so well-displayed as in the home-life of the nation . . . . With her new freedom come higher ambitions, nobler aspirations, loftier purposes. But whatever the path she chooses, however far she moves from her former confines, whatever the reforms she attempts, her central thought is home. All her plans look toward making that one spot as nearly perfect as possible."[63] A prosperous community, interested in its homes and eager to foster wholesome family life, offered the classical architects a chance to display their talent. Treat and Foltz, Frost and Granger, Horatio Wilson, Benjamin Marshall, W. Carbys Zimmerman, and Howard Van Doren Shaw, all of whom were or became prominent Chicago architects, designed houses in the area.

There were also those architects, many of whom were involved in the reform movement, who were determined to find a new, uniquely American, architectural expression, one that might be rooted in the past but would not imitate it. Among these were Hugh Garden, George Maher, Nimmons and Fellows, Dwight Perkins, Irving and Alan Pond, Robert Spencer, Tallmadge and Watson, and Frank Lloyd Wright.

Three Neighborhoods and Their Housing

It is tempting to consider Hyde Park–Kenwood as one neighborhood after annexation, but this is not possible. Although there was interaction among the three sections that had stretched out from the early Illinois Central stations, each continued to grow in its own way, and the differences remained greater than the similarities. They were all about the same size, a half-mile by about a mile and a quarter.

Kenwood. Of the three, Kenwood, being farthest from the site of the exposition, was the least affected physically by it. Its verdant isolation continued well into the nineties, when two important changes occurred. The first block of stores carrying food and household supplies was built on 47th Street at Lake Park Avenue in 1894. Though some homeowners protested, in time they found it convenient, and the new arrangement was welcomed by tradesmen who, until then, had been forced to deliver everything into the area by wagon. The second change, equally important, was the installation of the streetcar line on 47th Street, connecting

Kenwood for the first time with the West Side. It marked the end of 47th as a residential street and established a new boundary between north and south Kenwood.

The pattern of land use in Kenwood continued to be, in general, fairly uniform. Lots were large, houses set well back from the street, and row housing and apartments confined to the periphery. In 1893 the Illinois Supreme Court affirmed a lower court decision in the case of Charles Hutchinson and others against Russell Ulrich and W. I. Beman, permitting the latter two to continue construction of an apartment house on the southwest corner of Greenwood and 44th Street, the objection having been based on a clause in the deed calling for a single dwelling. The court ruled that an apartment building is a single dwelling, as opposed to a commercial structure.[64] Despite this ruling, there apparently was a strong enough feeling about multiple-family housing in Kenwood that not many apartment buildings were allowed to creep in. Property that looked as if it might be put to "undesirable development" was bought up by residents.[65]

Pl. 34

Although a few boulevard row houses, such as those built for C. A. Marshall by Horatio Wilson and O. W. Marble, appeared, these too tended to be at the edges rather than in the center of Kenwood. They seem to have been built in anticipation of an urbanization of Kenwood that never occurred.

John Dunham, who still held a large tract of land when he died in 1895, stipulated in his will that it not be sold until after the death of his last surviving heir. His heirs, the Hawes family, built a number of the houses on 50th Street, in Madison Park, and on Kimbark between 49th and 50th as rental properties. That part of Dunham's property remembered by oldtimers as "farmer's field" was never developed (cows were pastured there as late as the twenties). After the death of Dunham's daughter the land was bought by Albert Harris and set aside for what is now Shoesmith Park.

The people who lived in Kenwood during this period were white, Protestant, middle- and upper-class native Americans, much like the first group that had settled there, although in this period a few prosperous Jewish families were beginning to build. Homes were spacious, planned for large families and large staffs of servants. Their owners were businessmen: packers, wholesale grocers, lumber, coal, and iron dealers, utilities executives, clothing manufacturers, insurance men, and brokers. There were a few physicians and a number of lawyers. Women's occupations were listed in the 1900 census as "keeping house" or, for unmarried women, "at school" or "at home."

The architects can be roughly placed in three groups: traditional, innovative, and those who fall somewhere between. Probably the most tradition-bound was Henry Ives Cobb, who

Pl. 35

designed the first buildings for the University of Chicago. His Gothic house for Dr. J. A.

McGill, using the same Bedford stone he used for the university, was much admired for its fidelity to the style. Writing in *Inland Architect,* C. E. Jenkins observed, "The whole effect is most dignified and beautiful," illustrating "to a high degree how much can be done by following style. The slightest intrusion, the least attempt at the creative, would ruin the charming effect."[66]

Pl. 36   Less literal than Cobb, whose partner he had been from about 1884 to 1888, Charles Frost nevertheless drew upon historical forms. The house for John B. Lord, president of the Ayer and Lord Tie Company (manufacturers of railroad ties), freely combines massive bays, heavy window frames, slender pilasters, Palladian windows and dormers, using stone, copper, and terra cotta for the trim.

Pl. 37   Palladian windows are also a feature of the Gustavus Swift house, here combined with a number of other historic elements: Ionic columns supporting a broad verandah, second-floor bays with elaborate terra cotta ornamentation, and terra cotta griffins on shields blazoned with the letter *S.* Swift was the founder of the Swift Packing Company; his perfecting of the refrigerator car changed Chicago from a cattle shipping to a meat processing center. He and his family lived near the stockyards until they moved to Ellis avenue in 1898.[67] Like his close neighbors Martin Ryerson, Enos Barton, and Julius Rosenwald, he was a trustee and faithful supporter of the University of Chicago. His son, Harold, succeeded Martin Ryerson as president of the board of trustees. The architects for the Swift house were John J. Flanders and W. Carbys Zimmerman.

Pl. 38   Charles Frost went into partnership with Alfred Granger in 1898. One of the early fruits of this partnership was the three-story limestone mansion for Enos Barton, president of Western Electric. It is a smoothed-down, simplified version of a French chateau. The conservatory on the south was a frequent feature of Kenwood houses, as was the third-floor gymnasium.

Pl. 39   Zimmerman's partnership with Flanders was dissolved in 1898, and after that he practiced by himself. The house he built for C. A. Goodyear is notable for its elaborate stone ornamentation, the motif of which is echoed in the wrought-iron fence. Like Wright, Shaw, and others, Zimmerman was interested in the Arts and Crafts movement. The stonecutter for this house was John Tait.

Pl. 40   The neoclassical house for William T. Fenton, vice-president of the Bank of the Republic, has been variously attributed to Wilson, Wilson and Marshall, and Marshall. It was built as their partnership was ending, and it seems likely that it was Marshall's work. Its exaggerated opulence was to be an important characteristic of Marshall's building.

Pl. 41   More typical of the houses Horatio Wilson built in Kenwood (and he built a great many) is the residence for C. E. Scribner, chief engineer for Western Electric. Taking as his model

English domestic housing, Wilson designed solid, roomy, comfortable houses, adapted to the lives of large families. Less palatial than many in Kenwood, they nevertheless all had specially designed fireplaces and mosaic tile entrances. On Woodlawn Avenue alone he built six houses, contributing to the street's air of architectural unity.

It was not unusual for men to choose architects for their houses whom they knew through their industrial work. Joseph Schaffner, of Hart, Schaffner and Marx, selected William

Pl. 42   Holabird and Martin Roche, noted for their innovative and efficient office buildings and factories. The red-brick, Georgian house they designed for Schaffner, with its low wall, handsome portico, and evenly spaced windows and dormers, is simple yet massive. The sunporch is designed to catch all the available Chicago light.

All these houses appear to embody their owners' desire to identify with a prosperous, even lordly, past, and to look forward to a stable future. Built for family life and hospitality, they had large entrance or reception halls to welcome guests, spacious living and dining rooms, third-floor ballrooms and extensive servants' quarters.

Howard Van Doren Shaw built many if not most of his early houses in Hyde Park–Kenwood, several in Kenwood itself. He has been called the most liberal of the conservatives

Pl. 43   and the most conservative of the rebels.[68] The house he designed for Thomas E. Wilson, vice-president of the Morris Packing Company, reflects in its fine masonry, decorative stone trim, and stone urns Shaw's interest in creative craftsmanship.

Pl. 44   Like Shaw, Jarvis Hunt was a member of the informal club of progressive designers that met in Dwight Perkins's Steinway Hall offices. He built the massive, flat-roofed, three-story pressed-brick and stone house for Homer A. Stillwell. Its simple geometric forms receive their emphasis and ornamentation from the way the brick is used.

Among the innovators and architectural philosophers, those who articulated and shared their views on how to design and build, were Frank Lloyd Wright, Dwight Perkins, and George Maher.

Pls. 45, 46   At Kenwood and 49th are two of Frank Lloyd Wright's first houses. They were built in 1892, when Wright was working for Adler and Sullivan. He was well acquainted with the neighborhood, having courted his first wife, Catharine Tobin, who lived at 47th and Kimbark, while she was going to Hyde Park High School. In his autobiography Wright describes strolling with Catharine and looking at the new houses in Kenwood, "in the process of becoming the most fashionable of Chicago's residence suburbs."[69] Although Wright denied that there was anything clandestine about building these houses while he was working for Adler and Sullivan, the fact remains that the notices that appeared in May and June of 1892 in *The Economist*[70] attributed the houses to Wright's friend and colleague, Cecil Corwin.

However Wright felt about it, Adler and Sullivan considered his moonlighting a breach of contract, and Wright resigned or was fired, depending upon who tells the story. Although the two houses at first glance bear little resemblance to Wright's later Prairie School houses, they display an unmistakable originality—in the treatment of roof, porch, and windows in the Blossom house and in the modifications of the English style in the McArthur house. Wright's first attempts at designing leaded windows and his first use of the corner window are in the McArthur house, as well as his first work in designing interiors. In the Blossom coach house, on 49th Street, built in 1907, one can see the development of Wright's interest in the horizontal line.

Pl. 47

The brick house at 1120 East 48th Street was built by Dwight Perkins for J. J. Wait. From 48th Street only a little side porch can be seen. The house has to be viewed from the west; when it was first built it must have had a front lawn reaching all the way to Greenwood. The property originally belonged to Mrs. Charles Hitchcock, whose protégé Perkins was. Perkins expressed his philosophy of architecture in an interview shortly after this house was built. "I personally aim to mold mankind by building with reference to the common virtues, which are eternal. I mean by that, that when we build of brick we let it appear as brick. I do not attempt to imitate stone . . . . My buildings are planned so that ingress and egress are direct; so that the rooms relating to one another are connected; so that the rooms whose functions are private are separated; so that there is an abundance of light and air; and so that all modern conveniences are incorporated."[71]

Pl. 48

The house for Julius Rosenwald, of Sears, Roebuck and Company, by George C. Nimmons and William K. Fellows, displays the strong horizontal lines and Roman brick that characterized much of the Prairie School architecture. The house is ornamented only with delicate terra cotta molding and copper trim. Nimmons and Fellows, like Holabird and Roche, were industrial architects. Rosenwald thought it was practical to have the same architects for both plant and house.[72] It was planned to face south, and to overlook the garden, which was originally landscaped with a lily pond extending from the foot of the porch. Rosenwald was a moving force in the life of the city, indeed of the nation. He was a generous supporter of the University of Chicago, an active member of the city's reform groups, and an enlightened philanthropist. His program for educating black people established schools all over the South.

Pl. 49

Another Prairie School architect was George Maher, who designed the Magerstadt house. As in the Rosenwald house, the emphasis is on the horizontal line, enhanced by the use of the long Roman brick. One motif—the poppy—prevails throughout the decoration. It appears on the exterior stone carving, in the beautifully designed stained-glass windows, and in other interior details. Maher liked the idea of carrying one theme throughout. Like Wright and other Prairie School architects, he also designed furniture for his houses. Ernest Magerstadt, who was city collector at the time the house was built, and a power in the Republican party, gave Maher full rein.

Pl. 50

The two two-apartment buildings designed by George Maher in 1909 for E. Schoenfield, a lawyer, and Dr. Joseph De Lee, offer an interesting solution to the problems engendered by the pressure for multiple-family dwellings. In them we see the further development of Maher's own personal style. They are well-adapted to the street scene, gracing it with their individually designed facades.

Behind them the first private garage in Kenwood was built in 1910, by Hermann von Holst and James Fyfe. Some cars had probably been kept in coachhouses or public garages before this time, but this simple garage signaled a basic alteration in living patterns and introduced a new architectural entity—the size and shape, not to mention the care and feeding, of an automobile making very different demands on space from those of a horse and carriage.

Hyde Park Center. Of the three neighborhoods, Hyde Park Center grew most rapidly and least uniformly. It was separated from Kenwood by 51st Street, a boulevard, and from South Park by 55th Street with its streetcars and rows of stores and flats. It was bisected by 53d Street, where shops with offices and flats above them stretched westward from the original shopping nexus. From east to west it was further divided into three sections: east of the Illinois Central tracks, the central section, and the area west of Woodlawn Avenue.

East of the tracks the combination of the depression of the nineties and the oversupply of housing for the fair temporarily curtailed building on Hyde Park Boulevard, but in the late nineties large, substantially built city houses began to appear. They were often attached, or detached by only a few feet, and had narrow front yards. These were followed in the early 1900s by luxury apartment buildings. One of the first of these was designed to fit in with the

Pl. 51

single family residences on the boulevard. An investment property built by architects Frommann and Jebson, it boasted leaded stained-glass windows and an elaborately carved stone entrance, features that show it was intended for an elite clientele. Rows of other three-story apartments followed; most had front porches or sun rooms. The pattern is well illustrated in

Pl. 52

the line stretching south from 53d Street: two buildings designed by different architects, for the same developer. On Cornell, also, row houses and apartments were replacing the frame houses that had been built by the first settlers.

The middle portion of Hyde Park Center, from Lake Park Avenue west to Woodlawn Avenue, was traditionally the most densely populated of the neighborhood clusters. It was also the most heterogeneous, with the broadest income range and an assortment of ethnic groups.

The first and most fashionable street to be developed, Lake Park Avenue, was now extending its commercial reach north to 51st Street and south to 56th. By 1900 the big old houses on Lake Park had become boarding houses. The Chicago Beach Hotel and the Hyde Park Hotel employed black cooks, waiters, bellboys, and elevator men, many of whom with their families lived nearby on Lake Park.

Beyond, as far as Woodlawn, a tangle of row houses, six-flats, and suburban villas was going up. The row houses ran south from 51st Street on Dorchester and Blackstone. Suburban-type houses appeared on Kenwood between 52d and 53d, and on Harper between 54th and 55th. The house built by Samuel Treat and Fritz Foltz for O. M. Powers, who ran a business correspondence school, was, even at the time it was built, by far the most imposing on the street.

Wherever space was available, six-flats went up, squeezed in among the older housing. Blue-collar and white-collar workers, shopkeepers, schoolteachers, students, artists, musicians, and a few university professors lived here, in the old frame cottages, in boarding houses, and in the flats. Most were renters. In the area between 53d and 55th, Dorchester and Kimbark, the pattern of the seventies, which shows a concentration of immigrant laborers here, no longer existed. On Ridgewood Court in 1900, for instance, Swiss, French, English, Bohemians, Swedes, and blacks were living side by side with midwestern families—salesmen, clerks, bookkeepers, teachers, and an artist. Many of the women in this section were employed as salespeople, clerks, stenographers, dressmakers, milliners, teachers, and nurses. There was also a sprinkling of laundresses and domestic servants. Unlike Kenwood, where live-in servants were the rule, most of the households were servantless, unless they were boarding houses.[73]

West of Woodlawn, except for the 55th Street strip, density decreased abruptly, as if this area identified itself with Kenwood. Frank Lloyd Wright's house for packer Isidore Heller is now a historic landmark. Built only five years after the Blossom and McArthur houses, it shows the further development of Wright's concentration upon horizontality. The house is best viewed from the south, where the broad sweep of the roof and the decorative detail of the entry may be seen. The molded frieze by Richard Bock is a direct expression of Wright's interest in the Arts and Crafts movement.

During this period University Avenue, like Woodlawn, was just beginning to be developed with large single-family homes. Solon S. Beman designed the rough-cut gray stone house at 5317. Like the house down the street by James Gamble Rogers, it is neither entirely city nor entirely suburban. Both houses have a certain formality that is associated with city houses, but they are ample and free-standing, qualities more often found in the suburbs. Perhaps they

Pl. 53

Pl. 54

Pl. 55
Pl. 56

could be described as embodying the otherwise unacknowledged ambiguity that characterized this whole area.

Pl. 57

Candidly urban is the entire west side of the 5200 block on Greenwood, developed by S. E. Gross, one of Chicago's most active real estate operators, in partnership with Charles Counselman, a packer who lived at 51st and Greenwood. The houses, built by Gross's architect, are detached, though not by much. The roof line is continuous. Working within the limits of the street plan, the architect used a variety of traditional historical details to give each house individuality.

Pl. 58

On the western edge of Hyde Park Center, and adjacent to the southwest corner of Kenwood, still another Kenwood packer invested in a large apartment house by Horatio Wilson, among the first of many that would line 51st Street from Drexel Boulevard to the lake.

Much of the oldest and most heavily used housing of Hyde Park Center came down in the urban renewal program of the 1950s and 1960s. The boarding houses and cheap hotels that had been built for the fair had become verminous eyesores. The shops and saloons on Lake Park Avenue, the stores and flats on 55th and 53d had deteriorated into slums. They have been replaced by shopping centers, high-rise apartment buildings, row houses, and institutional complexes. But in their time they served an important purpose: they provided for a latitude of housing choices and services that vitalized the whole community from 47th to 59th. They supplied the "city" atmosphere that made the location attractive to the Baptists.

South Park: The University Community. If the fair stimulated a rise in property values close to the park, farther west the advent of the university also made them shoot up. Marshall Field's gift of ten acres to the university was no act of charity. He had paid $79,166 for sixty-three and a third acres in 1879, or about $1,253 an acre. As a result of his gift he was able to sell ten more acres to the university for $10,000 an acre. When Rockefeller made an additional gift of $1,000,000 for graduate studies and a Divinity School, assuring the institution's university status, it became clear that the original three-block site, between Ellis and Greenwood, 56th and 59th, would be inadequate. Negotiations were opened to exchange the northernmost block for one to the east, and to purchase a fourth block, making a square site running from 57th to 59th, Ellis to University. Marshall Field raised his price. President Harper, the trustees, and the Baptist Education Society fretted about whether or not they could meet it. In the end they did, buoyed up by the dream of the great university that would grow there.[74] To this original site, over the next eleven years, the university added $1,000,000 worth of property on both sides of the Midway from Cottage Grove Avenue to Dorchester.[75] One of the pieces, acquired by gift and purchase, was "Fernwood," the country estate of Jonathan Y. Scammon on 59th Street between Dorchester and Woodlawn.[76]

On the western edge of South Park was Cottage Grove Avenue. Like 55th Street, it had a car line. Also like 55th and its adjacent streets, it was an area of shops, low-rent cottages, and boarding houses. In 1900 the population included Irish, German, Swedish, Greek, Chinese, and black families—laborers, blacksmiths, teamsters, carpenters, tailors, dressmakers, railroad workers, clerks, students, artists, actors, and musicians. The Chicago Home for Incurables, on Ellis between 55th and 56th, housed about three hundred patients, and the people who cared for them lodged nearby on 55th and on Ellis and Ingleside. An auxiliary shopping area was developing on 57th Street, with a pharmacy and soda fountain, grocery store, home furnishings shop, cleaning establishment, and Chinese laundry.[77]

When the university opened, students were housed in both boarding houses and dormitories. Many of the faculty commuted long distances—from Morgan Park, even from the North Side. Others listed addresses in the first university directories in Switzerland, France, Greece, Germany, and Italy. Some faculty lived in the hotels and apartments that had been built for the fair. Others bought or rented houses south of the Midway or in the immediate neighborhood. Thomas W. Goodspeed, for instance, bought the little frame pre-fire house at 5630 Kimbark.

Within a very short time, however, faculty were buying lots on Woodlawn and University from Marshall Field, and lots on the streets to the east. Unlike Kenwood, where development ran from east to west, the main home-building activity began close to the campus on the west and then moved east onto streets that were already building up.

People in this community, reflecting the progressive stance of the university, tended to select young architects of the new school rather than such traditional and fashionable firms as Frost and Granger or Treat and Foltz. Certain bonds are discernible between some clients and their architects and between the architects themselves, which may account for the similarities in style and feeling apparent in the houses of this period. Howard Van Doren Shaw, who was just beginning his career as an architect, had been a friend at Yale of Professor George Vincent. Shaw built Vincent's house on University Avenue, and this commission led to many others. Irving and Allen Pond were the architects for Hull House; this brought them into contact with families like the Lillies, who also were committed to Hull House and its affairs. The Ponds were members of the Chicago Literary Club, to which Frederick Ives Carpenter and James Westfall Thompson, men for whom they built houses, also belonged. Dwight Perkins was the architect for the University of Chicago Settlement, to which Mrs. Russell Wiles devoted much of her time and energy. The young architects knew each other well; Hugh

Garden, Howard Shaw, Dwight Perkins, Frank Lloyd Wright, Vernon Watson, Thomas Tallmadge, Robert Spencer, and W. C. Zimmerman all met frequently and discussed and wrote about their own and each others' work.[78] This network of relationships and the closeness of the community, where many people shared ideas and friendships as well as a workplace, may explain the striking uniformity of the blocks closest to campus, a uniformity which, however, did not entail a sacrifice of individuality.

Pl. 59

Apartments and row houses slipped easily into this streetscape with no sense of city-suburban tension. One of the first buildings on Woodlawn was the apartment house by Irving and Allen Pond. Its diagonal lot placement, opening the apartments to light and air, the central stair tower, and the contrasting tones of the brick combine to present an original solution to the problems of the six-flat.

Pl. 60

The house built for three university bachelors, Frank Tarbell, Ernst Freund, and Joseph Iddings, is indistinguishable from the single-family residences on Woodlawn. In fact, it contained three separate apartments as well as shared common rooms.

Groups of professors also banded together and arranged for cooperative row housing. The New York firm of Mann, MacNeille, and Lindeberg did three such groups: one on Greenwood and 54th, one on 56th Street, and one on Kenwood Avenue. These houses, with their tiled roofs and leaded windows, present a single unified though varied facade. *Inland Architect* described them as a "unique and successful effort at cooperative building. While each house is being planned to suit the needs of the family which occupies it, the group as a whole forms a harmonious ensemble."[79]

Pl. 61
Pl. 62

Pl. 63

An ingenious variation on the row house occurs in the three houses Robert Spencer built on Blackstone. Though these houses are attached, the projecting fronts admit more air and light than do ordinary row houses. Spencer's interest in the decorative use of brick is apparent in the diaper pattern of lighter and darker brick running around the parapet wall.

Pl. 64

The professors' houses by Thomas Tallmadge and Vernon Watson carry the row house concept even further. The strong horizontal lines, accented by the vertical half-timbering, tie the structure together into one thoughtfully composed and integrated unit.

Pl. 65

The single-family houses show the architects, and presumably their clients, reaching for simplified forms and minimal historical decoration. The house built by Henry Ives Cobb for President Harper is a model of restraint compared with the chateau he designed for Dr. John A. McGill on Drexel Boulevard. With the president's house Cobb set a tone for residential architecture very different from that of the elaborate period pieces he designed for the campus. Though the steep gables echo the campus roofline, the house is built of Roman brick rather than Bedford stone, and there is no complicated Gothic ornamentation. (The house has been altered over the years; the porch on the Midway side has been removed and the entrance on University added.)

Two houses by Hugh Garden, a Prairie School architect, sustain this feeling of restraint.

Pl. 66

That for the classicist W. G. Hale, is an adaptation of the "Colonial" style with unusually delicate detail. The revival of this style was part of the attempt to break free from the bondage of European forms and work toward a truly American style. This house now faces north, which is unfortunate, for one rarely gets the play of light on its surfaces. Originally it was at 5757 University, but in the twenties it was put on rollers and moved.

Pl. 67

Garden's house for Robert Herrick, professor and novelist, is starkly rectangular and severe, and made even more so by the removal both of its shutters and of the leaded-glass windows on the first floor. Herrick's criticisms of Chicago's materialism in *The Web of Life* brought forth such violent reactions that he and Garden drastically simplified the original plans for the house.[80]

Pl. 68

Equally spare is the Dwight Perkins house for Mrs. Russell Wiles. "Plain almost to the verge of baldness," Robert Spencer described it, "the building is given a degree of interest by the grouping and proportion of the openings and its simple all-brick details."[81] This very plainness, this search for the essentials, was an underlying principle in the work of these young architects.

Pl. 69

More massive, yet also very simple in its basic outlines is the house for Dr. E. Fletcher Ingalls by Holabird and Roche, which also uses brick as the fundamental design unit. The house's vertical feeling is created by its steep pitched roof and the strong double chimney that rises with the house from its very base.

Pl. 70

Dr. E. O. Jordan's house has been attributed both to the Boston firm of Hartwell and Richardson and the Prairie School architect Myron Hunt. Hunt's name is on the permit. He may have been the Chicago representative for the Boston firm. Ths house itself shows a strong kinship with the work of other Chicago architects: the flat roof, the horizontal lines picked up in contrasting brick, the shallow arched recesses framing the windows. (A large porch was removed in the twenties). Dr. Jordan's research into the causes of typhoid fever gave impetus to the building of the Chicago Sanitary and Ship Canal, which reversed the course of the river, diverting Chicago's sewage from the lake.

Pl. 71

Even Patton and Fisher, an established, traditional Chicago firm, known for their Queen Anne houses and heavily Romanesque public buildings, simplified their forms for Professor H. H. Donaldson's house. It, too, is severely rectilinear, ornamented only by the Palladian windows and brick pilasters.

The lines of Howard Van Doren Shaw's houses were gentler. There are a number of these

Pl. 72
Pl. 73

Pl. 74

Pl. 75

Pl. 76

houses close to the campus as well as in Kenwood. His doorways were usually rounded, and he often used finely carved stone as decoration. The house for the great orientalist Edgar Goodspeed was said to be the last of Shaw's small houses. A. J. Mason's house is also by Shaw. Mason, who lived across the street from Dr. Jordan, was the inventor of the "grab," the mechanical crane and scooper used to dig the Sanitary and Ship Canal. Shaw was so well established in the university community that he was asked to build a house for Mrs. William Rainey Harper after her husband's death.

Like Shaw, Irving and Allen Pond were friends of but not followers of the Prairie School architects. Instead, they were developing their own distinctive style. The house for Professor James W. Thompson on Blackstone shows their interest in the various uses of brick and stone. The interior of the house is made lighter by substituting an open piazza for the overhanging porch.

The search for simplified forms, functional space, and expressive materials culminated in Frank Lloyd Wright's landmark house for Frederick Robie. It is a brilliant example of Prairie School architecture. Its long low lines, the abstract composition of its planes, and the engineering of the cantilevered roof make it one of Wright's great achievements. Every carefully worked out detail expresses Wright's unique vision of architecture and its relationship to peoples' lives: the leaded windows of clear and stained glass, the lighting fixtures, the interior furnishings. Totally midwestern, it had a worldwide influence on domestic architecture, freeing exterior treatment from the dictatorship of classical forms and interior space from the strictures of boxlike rooms. No house of equal importance had preceded the Robie house in Hyde Park–Kenwood, and assuredly none has succeeded it.

As these houses and apartments were going up in Kenwood, in Hyde Park Center, and in the university community, Chicago's businessmen, including many from the neighborhood, were sponsoring the efforts of Daniel Burnham and Edward H. Bennett to formulate a long-range plan for the city. Daniel Burnham had achieved major stature, locally, nationally, and internationally, both for his contributions to commercial architecture and his work as chief architect for the World's Columbian Exposition in 1893. His energy, his imaginative yet hard-headed approach to the solution of building problems, and the breadth and daring of his vision impressed Chicago's leaders of business and industry. Sensing the many difficulties that had been created in the course of the city's growth, the Commercial Club, whose membership included the wealthiest and most powerful men in town, asked Burnham to devise a blueprint for Chicago's future.

Fifty years separated Paul Cornell and Daniel Burnham, years in which Chicago grew rapidly and chaotically. The two men shared a faith that a good community was good for business, a feeling for the value of natural beauty in people's lives, and belief in a planned community. Both were operating at a time when the technology of communications was changing; the telephone and the automobile were altering Burnham's world as much as the telegraph and the railroad had altered Cornell's. Both men attacked their problems by writing to cities all over the world for advice.

But there the comparison stops. Cornell was able to start afresh; Burnham had to work with the old. In looking to the future he had to disentangle the haphazard skein of commercial and social relations that had found physical expression in Chicago's roadways and neighborhoods, working toward a plan that would rationalize them. Could Cornell, starting from scratch, have anticipated the explosive growth of his suburb? Could he have controlled or directed it? Would it have been a good thing if he had? The answer to all these questions is probably no, given all the conditions of nineteenth-century social and economic life. Perhaps it was only through its helter-skelter development, its triggered responses to changes in transportation, land values, commercial demands, fashions, movements, and ideas that this vital and heterogeneous neighborhood was able to grow.

Hyde Park–Kenwood is not embedded in a single decade of the past, nor is there uniformity of architecture. No one will ever call it quaint. Nor will any group try to reconstitute the old tavern at 56th and Lake Park Avenue and people it with barmaids in calico. The picture of its past as one strolls the streets is dynamic rather than static. Although as the neighborhood grew many of the original houses were burned or torn down to be replaced by newer, safer, more technologically advanced, more fashionable, or more profitable dwellings, the blocks that remain reveal the progress from suburban to urban living: the pre-fire houses on Dorchester; the Chicago cottages between 53d and 55th; the suburban villas on Kimbark and Kenwood south of 47th Street, and those on Harper Avenue south of 57th; the mansions of Chicago's business leaders; the professors' houses clustered around the university, and finally, the many three-story apartment buildings.

Through all these stages a strong emphasis on individuality is evident. Even the simplest of the Chicago cottages have special little variations in the wood trim, and most of the early row houses have individualized facades. Developers offered families choices as to room arrangements, exterior trim, interior fittings. "Will build to suit," said the advertisements for these houses. The more grandiose homes display a variety of styles ranging from historic to that of the uniquely midwestern Prairie School, reflecting not only the tastes of their owners but the training and philosophy of the architects. Among the latter were those who had learned through apprenticeships, a few who had been educated in the Midwest, and many who had studied in the East or in Europe.

There is no sense of tightness, restriction, or regulation. Rather, the houses of Hyde Park–Kenwood express the freedom and the eagerness to experiment with ideas, techniques, and materials that enlivened nineteenth- and early twentieth-century life.

Appendix A
Notes on the Architects

Hyde Park–Kenwood, during its growing years, provided a fertile field for architects of all persuasions. Even before the advent of the University of Chicago there were many residents who were interested in the arts, music, and the life of the mind. The university was a new and powerful stimulant, attracting around it members of an intellectual community. This influx, combined with the movement into Kenwood of highly successful industrialists, created a demand for single-family houses. There was also a ready market for multiple-family dwellings.

Many of the architects who built in the neighborhood also lived there or very close by: Solon S. Beman, W. I. Beman, Minard Beers, Arthur Cole, Frederick Foltz, George Nimmons, Reynolds Fisher, Benjamin Marshall, Thomas McCall, William Pruyn, Jr., Howard Van Doren Shaw, Samuel Treat, Horatio Wilson, and W. Carbys Zimmerman. Most were associated in other ways, through the Chicago Architectural Club, the Arts and Crafts Society, and other groups interested in architecture.

What follows is a list of architects from whom we have three or more existing dwellings built before the end of 1910. The date given is that of the first notice. An asterisk denotes an apartment building. A number of the architects listed, including Alschuler, Holsman, Spencer, Pond and Pond, Schmidt and Garden, Borst and Hetherington, and Newhouse, of course, continued to design buildings in the neighborhood after 1910. I have made no attempt to discriminate among architects or buildings on the basis of merit. In many instances it might have been tempting to single out inspired work and ignore more humdrum buildings. But in a survey of this sort, which stresses community development, the picture would be distorted if only the best architects and most important buildings were included.

Alfred Alschuler (1876–1940)

LOCATION	OWNER	DATE
4907 Greenwood	Louis A. Kohn	1906
4921 Ellis	Julius Weil	1907
5009 Ellis	David Yondorf	1908

Although Alschuler was still in his early thirties when he built these houses on Greenwood and Ellis, he had already been elected president of the Chicago Architectural Club. He was born and raised in Chicago, educated at South Division High School and at Armour Institute, where he got his BS and MS degrees in 1899 and 1900. He went into the firm of Treat and Adler, and later entered into a partnership with Treat, the firm becoming Treat and Alschuler. In 1907 he went into practice by himself.[1] He designed many office and industrial buildings, and was also the architect for Isaiah Israel Temple (now KAM–Isaiah Israel).

Minard LeFever Beers (1847–1918)

5411 Harper	L. A. Barstow	1889
5318 Blackstone	David Quigg	1890
5410 Harper	C. M. Oughton	b. 1890

Beers, Clay and Dutton

5247 University	Robert Smith	1891
1501–03 Dorchester		1892

Beers was born in Ohio in 1847. His father was a builder and named his son after the French architect and writer Minard LeFever, known in this country for his *Modern Builders' Guide* (1833); *Beauties of Modern Architecture* (1835); and *The Architectural Instructor* (1856). His father's ambitions for him being apparent from birth, Beers learned carpentry at home and then studied with Joseph Ireland, an architect in Cleveland, Ohio. Arriving in Chicago in 1871, he worked as a draughtsman for Otis Leonard Wheelock, and then went into partnership with Oscar Cobb for a few years. When he came to Hyde Park in 1877 he went into practice on his own.[2] He built a number of houses in the area as well as schools and other public buildings. Unfortunately, only a very few examples of his work remain; unpretentious, simple family homes, dating from the late eighties and early nineteies, they are representative of a much larger number, now demolished.

Solon S. Beman (1853–1919)

5732 Harper	F. Reynolds	1884
5824 Harper	John Jackman, Jr.	1884
5832–5834 Harper	John Jackman, Jr.	1884
5759 Harper	F. D. Reynolds	1884
5708 Harper	J. C. Cook	1884
4935 Greenwood	E. Turner	1888
1019 E. 48th	D. O. Strong	1888
5317 University	Alice W. Tomlinson	1904

Beman was born in Brooklyn, New York, in 1853. When he was seventeen he entered the offices of the well-known New York architect, Richard Upjohn, where he studied for eight years. He practiced independently in New York for two years; then George M. Pullman brought him to Chicago and commissioned him to build the town of Pullman.[3] It was after he had built Pullman that he undertook to supervise the design of the houses in Rosalie Court (Harper Avenue between 57th and 59th). More elaborate are the houses on Greenwood and on University avenues. Classical in feeling, heavy, and substantial, these houses reflect Beman's lifelong interest in Greek architecture, an interest which is also apparent in the Blackstone Library and Christian Science Church on Dorchester and 48th Street (now the Shiloh Missionary Baptist Church).

W. Irving Beman and Ferdinand Parmentier

5200, 5202 Kimbark	Atwood Vane	1889
1353–55–57–59 E. 50th	J. H. Dunham	1890
1321–25–27 E. 51st	W. I. Beman	1890
5000–02–04 Blackstone		1892

W. I. Beman

5744 Harper	E. W. Heath	1886
5228 Kenwood	W. I. Beman	1889
5222 Kenwood	W. I. Beman	1889
5142 Blackstone	H. C. Allen	1892

W. Irving Beman, who was a brother of Solon, and Parmentier, a French émigré, were both in the architectural offices of Pullman, where Parmentier was a draftsman.[4] In the late eighties and early nineties Beman and Parmentier built a number of houses in Hyde Park–Kenwood. Some were of frame construction, but most were brick and stone row houses, erected as investment properties. In 1893 Parmentier left for California, terminating the partnership.

Bishop & Co.

5842–44 Harper*	C. D. Armstrong	1902
5641 Woodlawn	C. W. Hoff	1905
5431–37 Woodlawn*		1909
4800–10 Dorchester*	C. W. Hoff	1909
5046 Greenwood		1910

The son of a builder, Thomas A. Bishop specialized in apartment houses, one of his clients being C. W. Hoff, Hyde Park banker and real estate broker.[5]

George H. Borst (1848–1917) and John Todd Hetherington (1858–1936)

5421 Hyde Park Boulevard (Borst)	Emily C. Weeks	1901
5657–59 Woodlawn	James Rankin	1902
5450 Hyde Park Boulevard	R. S. Thompson	1902
5327 University	J. H. McNamara	1907

Hetherington was born and educated in Scotland. When he first came to Chicago he worked in the firm of Treat and Foltz.[6] This firm produced solid, well-built, commodious brick houses with pleasant interior detail.

Joseph C. Brompton

5200–44 Greenwood	S. E. Gross	1903

Gross was one of Chicago's most energetic real estate developers, and Brompton was his architect. Gross developed a plan of purchasing large pieces of property, subdividing them, building houses on them, and selling the houses for monthly payments.[7] Brompton designed many of his development houses, introducing a classically derived variety into their facades.

Henry Ives Cobb (1859–1931)

4938 Drexel	J. A. McGill	1891
5855 Woodlawn	William Rainey Harper	1894
5630 Woodlawn	W. C. Wilkinson	1896

Cobb is best known in the neighborhood as the designer of the first buildings in the University of Chicago complex.[8] Although he built only three private houses, his influence on neighborhood architecture was extensive. The strong Gothic style of the campus formed a backdrop for houses whose designs were derived from English prototypes. English domestic architecture was considered by many to be most appropriate to both American needs and the campus scene. Even at some distance from the campus the influence of the style can be seen in the heraldic devices that ornament many houses and apartment buildings.

A. W. Cole

5413 Greenwood	A. W. Cole	1898
5411 Greenwood	E. E. Hill	1898
5407 Greenwood	A. F. Webster	1902

Cole and Dahlgren

5201–09 Kenwood	C. H. Root	1888
5736–38 Blackstone	H. H. Belfield	1888
5210 Kenwood	G. W. Hoyt	1892

Like M. L. Beers and W. I. Beman, A. W. Cole built in the vernacular, both nicely designed row houses, each with an individual touch, and homey Queen Anne villas.

Jacob F. and John P. Doerr

5330 University	Mary A. Hearn	1900
5008–14 Dorchester*	William Doerr	1902
5216–18 Dorchester*	W. L. De Beck	1902
5000–04 Dorchester*		1902
1369–71 E. 50th*		1902
5201–09 Blackstone*	William Doerr	1904
5213–15 Dorchester	Joseph Schmidt	1904
4932, 4936 Kimbark	William Morris	1906

5443–45 Cornell*	Harry F. Morris	1908
5487–99 Hyde Park Boulevard*	William Doerr	1908
4933 Dorchester*	Henry Peterson	1909
5427–29 Hyde Park Boulevard*	Harry F. Morris	1910
5478–84 Everett*	William Doerr	1910
4915, 4919 Woodlawn	William H. Morris	1910

The Doerr brothers were prolific builders of apartment houses, their chief clients being William and Harry Morris, who were in the sash and door business, and a third brother William Doerr, also an architect. Gilbert and Bryson, in *Chicago and Its Makers,* claim that William Doerr was to modern Hyde Park what Paul Cornell was to the pioneer settlement, taking a major role in transforming the village into an outlying residential area of the city. Doerr's Hyde Park activities started in 1890 and continued into the late twenties. What we see in this listing is only the beginning of a series of apartment buildings, hotels, and apartment hotels.[9] The Doerr brothers built substantial, roomy apartments in a period when much that was done was cheap and shoddy. Many of their buildings are identical, or distinguished only by slight variations in the facades. Their apartment buildings were all of three stories, typically containing six apartments, though some were much larger. The average cost of construction was about $30,000, or $5,000 per apartment.

John J. Flanders (1874–1914) and W. Carbys Zimmerman (1859–1932)

5611 Blackstone	W. C. Zimmerman	1886
5621 Blackstone	W. C. Zimmerman	1886
4830 Kenwood	C. Matthews	1892
4848 Ellis	G. F. Swift	1898

W. Carbys Zimmerman

4840 Greenwood	C. A. Goodyear	1902
4841 Woodlawn	F. K. Hoover	1906
5001 Ellis	W. M. Crilly	1908
4940 Woodlawn	Frank B. Stone	1908
5633 Woodlawn	R. West	1909
5707 Woodlawn	W. B. Wolff	1909
4906 Greenwood	W. O. Johnson	1910

Flanders was one of the architects who helped rebuild Chicago after the fire. Like many of Chicago's early architects, his only preparation was a high school education. He served as an apprentice in the offices of Augustus Bauer, W. W. Boyington, and Edward Burling and Dankmar Adler, ultimately forming his own firm of Furst and Flanders, a partnership that lasted only four years. The Mallers Building, built in 1884–85 by Flanders, was one of Chicago's earliest skyscrapers, the first twelve-story structure in the city.[10] The partnership with Zimmerman was formed in 1886, after Zimmerman had received his training at Massachusetts Institute of Technology and worked in the offices of Burnham and Root. The firm designed a large number of schools and residences. The partnership terminated in 1898, and Zimmerman went into practice for himself in Steinway Hall.[11] Zimmerman's classical education is apparent in his work, but in no way restricts it.

Charles Frost (1856–1932) and Alfred Hoyt Granger (1867–1939)

4801 Drexel	Moses Born	1901
4920 Greenwood	Enos Barton	1901
4927 Drexel (coach house)	Simon Mandel	1902
4847 Woodlawn	W. F. Burrows	1902

Charles Frost

4810 Ellis	J. C. Hutchins	1894
4800 Ellis	E. C. Potter	b. 1896
4857 Greenwood	John B. Lord	1896

After studying at MIT, Charles Frost went into partnership with Henry Ives Cobb from about 1884 until 1888, during the period when the firm constructed the Chicago Opera House (now demolished).[12] Granger also studied at MIT and for two years at the Ecole des Beaux Arts in Paris. He spent several years as a draftsman in the offices of Shepley, Rutan and Coolidge, both in Boston and Chicago, and later worked in the offices of Jenney and Mundie in Chicago.[13] Frost and Granger became partners in 1898; they were brothers-in-law, both having married daughters of Marvin Hughitt, president of the North Western Railway. Predictably, they were also architects for the railroad and became experts in station design. Like Cobb, they were traditionalists in their domestic architecture. They were not, however, as literal as Cobb; they handled the different architectural styles more freely.

Hugh M. G. Garden (1873–1961)

5727 University	W. G. Hale	1897
5737 University	Robert Herrick	1901
4825 Woodlawn (Richard Schmidt)	Lester Frankenthal	1902

Born and educated in Canada, Garden worked for Flanders and Zimmerman when he first came to Chicago. Later he went into practice on his own, but at the same time he designed for Richard Schmidt, who was primarily an engineer. Garden and Schmidt finally entered into a partnership, Schmidt, Garden and Martin, in 1907. Garden was a gifted draftsman who made drawings for Sullivan and Adler as well as Schmidt. He was one of the group of Chicago architects who were striving to find an American idiom, freed from the fashions dictated by Europe and the past.[14]

William Holabird (1854–1923) and Martin Roche (1855–1927)

4819 Greenwood	Joseph Schaffner	1904
5637 Woodlawn	Lucius Teter	1905
5540 Woodlawn	E. Fletcher Ingalls	1905
5036 Ellis	Henry C. Hart	1910

Holabird and Roche were both trained in William Le Baron Jenney's office. Best known for their contributions to the commercial architecture of the Chicago school, they were responsible for many utilitarian and structural solutions in building, using a systematic scientific approach to the problems of construction and functional design.[15] Apparently they did relatively few houses, so it is interesting to find four, all in good condition, in Hyde Park–Kenwood.

Henry K. Holsman (1866–1960)

5124 Cornell	A. B. Mulvey	1898
5537 Woodlawn	George M. Eckels	1899
5733 University	C. D. Buck	1901

W. L. Brainerd and H. Holsman

5130 Cornell	A. B. Mulvey	1897
5138–40 Cornell	A. B. Mulvey	1897

The partnership between Brainerd and Holsman lasted only from 1893 to 1897. It appears that Holsman was the chief designer. His red brick houses show a sensitive use of the building material. A further claim to distinction is the "Holsman" automobile, which he designed and patented in 1900, the first two-cylinder automobile in America. After 1910 he built a number of cooperative apartment houses in Hyde Park–Kenwood.[16] He was the designing member of the real estate firm of Parker, Holsman.

Thomas McCall (1857–1925)

5553–35 Blackstone*	M. R. Potter	1902
5716–18 Dorchester*	George Low	1903
5427–33 Harper*	John A. Carroll	1905
5541 University	T. G. Soares	1906
5642 Kimbark*	E. Washburne	1906
5046–56 Blackstone*	Joseph Cormack	1906
1356–60 E. 58th*		1907
5413–15 Cornell*		1907
5536 Kimbark*	Rudolph Bobb	1908
5527–29 Cornell*	John W. Coutts	1909
5631–37 Dorchester*		1909
5557–59 Blackstone*		1909
5400–02 Dorchester*		1909
4933 Dorchester*	Henry Peterson	1909
5756–58 Kenwood*	F. E. Livengood	1910

Born in Scotland, McCall had his early architectural experience in London. He came to Chicago in 1891 and immediately plunged into designing hotels to accommodate World's Fair visitors. He continued to work in Hyde Park–Kenwood where he built a large number of apartment houses, many of which still stand; some were two-story flats, but most were the three-story six-flat buildings so characteristic of the period and neighborhood.[17]

George W. Maher (1864–1926)

5518 Hyde Park Boulevard	W. B. Conkey	c. 1889
5522 Hyde Park Boulevard	N. Anderson	c. 1889
5517, 5519 Cornell	A. F. Shuman	1889
5533, 5535, 5537 Cornell	A. F. Shuman	1889

5482, 5484 Hyde Park Boulevard	D. Johnson and L. P. Perry	1892
4807 Greenwood	J. J. Dau	b. 1897
4930 Greenwood	E. J. Magerstadt	1908
5024, 5028 Ellis*	E. Schoenfeld, J. De Lee	1909

One of the architects who strove to break loose from precedent and develop a new freedom in form and building, George Maher designed many unusual and compelling houses. He was searching for an architectural expression based on democracy, truth, and indigenous development, free of stylistic reminiscences. Born in West Virginia, he came to Chicago at the age of thirteen and began to study architecture in the well-established firm of Bauer and Hill. From there he went to Joseph Lyman Silsbee's office, one of the largest in the city, where he was soon joined by Frank Lloyd Wright. Maher left Silsbee's office in 1888, and before long went into partnership with Cecil Corwin, a relationship that ended about 1893. Maher was one of the most productive members of the Prairie School. Like Shaw, Wright, Perkins, and Spencer he was very much involved in the Arts and Crafts movement. Maher's work in this neighborhood ranged over a twenty-year period, which makes possible interesting comparisons between the early and later periods.[18]

Horace B. Mann (1868–1937), Perry R. MacNeille (1872–1937) and Lindeberg

5309, 5315, 5317, 5319 Greenwood	Professors' houses	1904
1220, 1222, 1226, 1228 E. 56th, 5558 Kimbark	Professors' houses	1904
5601, 5603, 5605, 5607 Kenwood 1351, 1357, 1361 E. 56th Street	Professors' houses	1905
5714 Woodlawn	F. R. Mechem	1905

Argyle Robinson

5757 Kimbark	W. G. Hale	1908
1308 E. 58th Street	J. P. Hall	
5714–24 Kenwood*	John B. Jackson	1909

Mann, MacNeille, and Lindeberg, a New York firm, opened an office in Chicago while these houses were being built. Mann's brother Charles, a professor at the University of Chicago, was probably responsible for the firm's first commission for professors.[19] Argyle Robinson eventually became the Chicago representative of the firm. A graduate of Hyde Park High School, he received his training at Armour Institute and MIT, and started a general practice in Chicago in 1900.[20]

Benjamin Marshall (1874–1944) and Charles Fox (1870–1926)
See also *Wilson and Marshall*

4930 Woodlawn	Walden D. Shaw	1907
5825 Blackstone*	Frederick Bode	1909

Marshall must have had a natural gift for design and engineering, for he had no formal architectural education. After graduating from the Harvard School (now Harvard–St. George) in Kenwood, he worked as an office boy in a clothing firm. At nineteen he went to work for Horatio Wilson, and by the time he was twenty-one he had become a partner in the firm. The partnership lasted seven years, after which Marshall went into practice alone. In 1905 he opened an office with Charles Fox. Trained in both civil engineering and architecture, Fox had been with Holabird and Roche before joining Marshall. In addition to numerous commercial buildings, the firm designed the South Shore Country Club, several theaters, and Chicago's most lavish hotels, the Drake, the Blackstone, and (now demolished) the Edgewater Beach.[21]

Henry Newhouse (1874–1929)

5020 Ellis	A. Hoefield	1908
5728–30 Drexel*	Emanuel Winter	1908
5125 Ellis*	Andrew Harper	1910
5237–45 Kenwood*	Collins & Morris	1909

Newhouse received his architectural education at MIT. His work in this neighborhood extends over several decades. From a later period, after 1910, we still have the Cooper-Carlton Hotel (now the Del Prado) and KAM Temple (now PUSH headquarters).[22]

George C. Nimmons (1865–1947) and William K. Fellows (1870–1948)

George Nimmons

4851 Kenwood	E. G. Chase	1898
4820 Kenwood	G. Fellows	1899

George Nimmons and William Fellows

5757, 5759 Blackstone	Katharine Rush	1899
4901 Ellis	Julius Rosenwald	1903
4823 Kenwood	Platt P. Gibbs	1904

This firm was formed in 1899, after Nimmons had worked for Burnham and Root, assuming responsibility for much of Root's work following the latter's death. Fellows had completed a course in architecture at Columbia University, after which he became an instructor in design in the new Chicago School of Architecture at the Art Institute. The firm did industrial work primarily; like the firm of Holabird and Roche it was chiefly interested in the solution of structural and utilitarian problems.[23]

W. A. Otis (1855–1929)

4917 Greenwood	Charles E. Gill	1896
4923 Greenwood	L. A. Carton	1896
1219 E. 50th	L. D. Kellog	1905

William Le Baron Jenney (1832–1907) and W. A. Otis

4747 Kimbark	W. R. Page	1886

A native of New York state, Otis was educated in architecture at the University of Michigan and, later, in France, at the Ecole des Beaux Arts. When he came to Chicago he served as a draftsman in Jenney's office. In 1886 he became a partner in the firm of Jenney and Otis; this partnership lasted three years, after which Otis went into practice alone. Otis's most important contribution to the community was the Hull Memorial Chapel for the First Unitarian Society at 57th and Woodlawn.

Jenney was born in Massachusetts and studied engineering in France. He came to Chicago in 1867 after serving as an engineer in the Civil War. He became a leading Chicago architect, applying engineering solutions to the problems of commercial building. Many Chicago architects were trained in his firm, including Sullivan, Holabird, Roche, and Burnham.[24]

5317–43 Harper*	Henry Phipps	1908

This large apartment building was erected after Jenney's death, but while the firm still retained his name.

Normand Smith Patton (1852–1915) and Reynolds Fisher

4734 Kimbark	Reynolds Fisher	b. 1890
4801 Kimbark	J. H. Howard	1891
5740 Woodlawn	H. H. Donaldson	1895

Patton had a long history of working for government agencies as an architect, both in Washington and in Chicago. In Chicago he was for some years architect for the board of education. Fisher was with the firm a relatively short time, withdrawing to return to Detroit. Patton built not only school buildings, but libraries and museums. The firm did the initial plans for the First Baptist Church in Hyde Park (now the Hyde Park Union Church).[25]

Dwight Heald Perkins (1867–1941)

1120 E. 48th	J. J. Wait	1897
4914 Greenwood (with H. H. Waterman)	Robert Vierling	1899
5711 Woodlawn	Russell Wiles	1901

If the architects who designed and built for this community can be divided into those who treated their work purely as a business proposition and those who intellectualized their role, Dwight Perkins must surely fall in the latter category. He was a member of a small but increasingly influential group who tried in their work to enrich people's lives. His school buildings, for which he became famous, were designed to provide for the city's children, particularly the sons and daughters of the immigrant poor, all that might be lacking in their homes. Born in Memphis, Tennessee, he grew up in Chicago. After graduating from MIT and teaching there for a year, he returned to Chicago and entered the office of Burnham and Root. He began to practice independently in 1894. One of his early projects was Steinway Hall, where he had offices which he shared with Myron Hunt, Robert Spencer, and Frank Lloyd Wright. He was an active and articulate participant in the movement toward a new, indigenous architecture, seeking above all truthfulness in the use of materials and the beauty that comes from the utility of the structure.[26]

Frederick Perkins (1866–1928)

4832 Ellis	Alonzo M. Fuller	1890
4921 Dorchester	A. H. Trotter	1890
4840 Ellis	Frank Fuller	1891
4860 Kimbark	Norman Carroll	1898

Born in Burlington, Wisconsin, Perkins studied in Wisconsin and then went to MIT. Following this, he studied at the Ecole des Beaux Arts in Paris. He came to Chicago in the late eighties and became, during the nineties, a prominent society architect.[27] His most spectacular work was probably the John G. Shedd mansion, designed in the French Gothic style, at 4515 Drexel Boulevard (now demolished).

Irving K. Pond (1857–1939) and Allen B. Pond (1858–1929)

5751, 5755 Harper (Irving Pond)	Irving Pond	1885
5515 Woodlawn	J. A. Miller	b. 1894
5117, 5119 Dorchester	Wheeler and Goldsmith	1895
5531 Woodlawn	F. I. Carpenter	b. 1899
5747 Blackstone	J. W. Thompson	1899
5222 Hyde Park Boulevard	John S. Coonley	1900
5801 Kenwood	Frank R. Lillie	1902
5625 Woodlawn	Charles H. Miller	1910

Like Dwight Perkins, the Pond brothers were concerned with both the social and aesthetic aspects of architecture. They were closely connected with the Hull House movement, and over the years they designed and built both the Hull House complex and Chicago Commons, making a serious study of the special problems of settlement house buildings. Like Perkins, too, they found their ornament in the way the building material, particularly brick, was used. Strongly antitraditionalist, they nevertheless were not allied with the Prairie School. Although they were among the group of architects in Steinway Hall and members of the architect's luncheon club, Irving Pond, the real designer of the firm, rejected the tenets of the Prairie School.[28] Both brothers were active in public affairs and literary organizations as well as the architectural associations. They were members of the City Club, the Little Room, and the Literary Club. The Congregational church they built at Dorchester and 56th is long since gone, but the American School of Correspondence still stands at 58th and Drexel, as does the Lorado Taft Studio at 60th and Ellis.

William H. Pruyn, Jr.

5441, 5445 Hyde Park Boulevard	Wheeler and Goldsmith	1897
1316 Madison Park	Kirk Hawes	1898
1323–27–31 E. 50th	J. D. Hawes	1901
4933, 4941 Kimbark	Kirk Hawes	1902
1310 Madison Park	Kirk Hawes	1902
4948 Kimbark	D. Hawes	1903
4928 Kimbark	Kirk Hawes	1903
4926 Kimbark	H. B. Leavitt	1906
4901 Kimbark	E. A. Graff	1906
931–49 E. 51st*		1910

The son of a contractor who worked for Horatio Wilson, Pruyn, like many sons of builders at that time, became an architect, specializing in investment properties.

Charles W. Rapp (1860–1927) and George L. Rapp (1878–1941)

5725 Woodlawn	George C. Howland	1900
5729 Woodlawn	John A. Roche	1901
5430 Cornell	J. Frank McKinley	1908
5437–39 Cornell*	C. L. Anderson	1909

Rapp and Rapp were to become famous for their elaborate, fantasy-laden movie theaters: the Tivoli at 63d and Cottage Grove was one of their creations. In the twenties they also built the "new" Windermere, still standing on East 56th Street.[29]

Andrew Sandegren (1869–1924)

1352–54 E. 48th*	Frank Gustafson	1901
5227–29 Dorchester*	C. T. Hallgren	1905
4816–28 Dorchester*	Claus Carlson	1906
5474–80 Hyde Park*	Frank Gustafson	1906
4715–21 Greenwood*	Charles Hallgren	1907
1358–64 E. 48th*		1908
5310–22 Hyde Park*	Sherman Cooper	1909
5411–13 Hyde Park*	M. Anderson	1910
5457–59 Hyde Park	Charles Anderson	1910

A specialist in apartment houses, Sandegren built a great many, both in Hyde Park–Kenwood and in other locations all over Chicago. Most of those in this area were family apartments of eight, nine, or ten rooms.

Howard Van Doren Shaw (1869–1926)

5533 Hyde Park Boulevard	Henry Thompson	1895
4911 Greenwood	Cornelia McLaury	1896
5337 University	George E. Vincent	1897
4901 Woodlawn	Charles Starkweather	1902
5724 Kimbark	W. S. Jackman	1903
4924 Woodlawn	Morris Rosenwald	1903
5533 University	O. Bolza	1904
5715 Woodlawn	A. J. Mason	1904
5539 Woodlawn	B. A. Streich	1905
5706 Woodlawn	Edgar Goodpseed	1906
5730 Kimbark	Mrs. W. D. Jackman	1907
4830 Woodlawn	James Douglas	1907
5728 Woodlawn	Mrs. William R. Harper	1907
5744 Kimbark	Charles G. Eaton	1907
4900 Greenwood	Henry Veeder	1907
5615 Woodlawn	B. W. Sippy	1909
4815 Woodlawn	Thomas E. Wilson	1910

Hyde Park and Kenwood abound in examples of the early work of Shaw. A graduate of Yale and MIT, Shaw was well-acquainted with all aspects of building. His office was a one-man operation and he personally supervised all his houses. Shaw was a great admirer of William Morris and helped form the Arts and Crafts Society in Chicago. His houses, which are adaptations of the English country house, are characterized by stone carving, rounded doorways, and a pleasant, restful composition of surfaces. He was capable of a great range of designs, from those for very small houses to imposing mansions.[30] In addition to the private houses, he designed several fraternity houses, the present Quadrangle Club, and the Church of the Disciples.

Robert C. Spencer, Jr. (1864–1953)

5719, 5721, 5723 Blackstone	W. S. Whiton	1896

Spencer, too, went to MIT, after which he worked in the offices of Shepley, Rutan and Coolidge. He was a close friend of Wright and associated with the other Prairie School architects. Like Wright, Perkins, and Shaw he was a moving force in the Arts and Crafts movement. His articles for *Brickbuilder* and for *House Beautiful* deal with the theory and practice of domestic architecture.[31]

Clarence Stiles and John Stone

5332, 5324 Blackstone	W. S. Johnson	1891
5723–37 Kenwood	Walter C. Nelson	1893
5732 Kenwood	Nicholas Hunt	1893
5762 Harper	Emma Over	1894

John Stone

5626–38 Blackstone	Lucy Norton	1898
5335 Harper*	J. M. Marshall	1898
5701–09 Kenwood*	Walter Nelson	1898
1355–57–59–61 E. 57th		
5740 Kimbark	F. G. Wright	1905
5700–10 Kimbark*		1910
1227–29 E. 57th		

Apartment buildings and row houses were the specialty of this firm. They were very much in the urban tradition of the period; in fact Stone's contractor, H. Bernritter, was able to master the style so well that the gray stone row houses he erected (5801–09 Blackstone and 5434 and 5438 Cornell) are indistinguishable from Stone's.

Thomas E. Tallmadge (1876–1940) and Vernon Watson (1879–1950)

5601–09 Woodlawn		
1215–17 E. 56th	Professors' houses	1908

Tallmadge, a graduate of MIT, and Watson, who had trained at Armour Institute in Chicago, became acquainted while both were working in the office of D. H. Burnham. They formed their own firm in 1905. Tallmadge, in addition to being an architect himself, was a teacher and a brilliant and perceptive architectural historian. It was he who coined the term "Chicago School." Tallmadge and Watson were closely associated with the members of the Prairie School, with whom they exhibited in the annual shows of the Chicago Architectural Club, and Tallmadge was the Prairie School's most devoted historian.[32]

Samuel A. Treat (1839–1910) and Frederick Foltz (1843–1916)

4851 Drexel	Martin A. Ryerson	1887
4801 Kenwood	H. S. Cutler	1888
5120 Kimbark	C. S. Dennis	1889
5730 Kenwood	W. P. Patterson	1889
5416 Harper	O. M. Powers	1892
5026 Greenwood	W. O. Goodman	1892
5022 Greenwood	George A. Tripp	1892
5130 University	E. E. Chandler	1895

Treat and Foltz was one of the oldest and most successful Chicago firms.

As in many other firms, there was a division of labor, Treat handling the practical problems and Foltz acting as designer. Foltz was born in Germany and studied and practiced there until 1866, when he came to New York. He came to Chicago in 1868 and practiced alone until he was burned out by the fire. In 1872 he joined Treat in a partnership that lasted until 1896. During this period the firm built residences, factories, and public buildings.[33]

Horatio Wilson (1857–1917) and Benjamin Marshall (1874–1944)
See also Benjamin Marshall and Charles Fox

4932 Ellis	H. R. Wilson	1899
4950 Ellis	H. M. Wilcox	1899
5009 Greenwood	D. W. Bremner	1899
4900 Ellis	B. H. Marshall	1899
4745 Ellis	W. T. Fenton	1899
4906 Ellis	Benjamin Marshall	1899
4845 Ellis	E. H. Phelps	b. 1902

Horatio Wilson

4929 Woodlawn	C. E. Scribner	1906
4905 Woodlawn	Fred A. Price	1906
4925 Woodlawn	B. H. Conkling	1907
4943 Woodlawn	George Birkhoff, Jr.	1907
4945 Woodlawn	George Birkhoff, Jr.	1907
4900 Woodlawn	A. W. Wolfe	1908
5100 Hyde Park Boulevard*	E. and J. P. Smith	1909
5100–16 Ellis		
5324–30 Hyde Park Boulevard*		1910
4918 Kimbark	F. E. White	1910
949–53 Hyde Park Boulevard*	G. Freund	1910
4805 Drexel	George B. Robbins	1910

Wilson came to Chicago in 1877 and studied architecture under a private tutor. He became one of Chicago's most popular and most prolific architects. He not only built a large number of houses, but he also designed banks, theaters, and factories.[34]

Frank Lloyd Wright (1867–1959)

4852 Kenwood	Warren McArthur	1892
4858 Kenwood	George Blossom	1892
5132 Woodlawn	I. Heller	1897
1332 E. 49th	Blossom Coach House	1907
5757 Woodlawn	Frederick Robie	1908

When Wright first came to Chicago from Madison, Wisconsin, he worked for a short time in the office of Joseph Lyman Silsbee. From there he went to the offices of Adler and Sullivan, where he remained for five years, leaving to go into practice for himself.

Wright became the leading genius and spokesman for the Prairie School. His influence was not only local but national and international. In freeing interior living space from the confines of boxlike rooms he changed the entire concept of the American home. Few of those who imitated him had his genius for design, however, and it is this that makes his houses so remarkable today.[35]

Hyde Park Houses

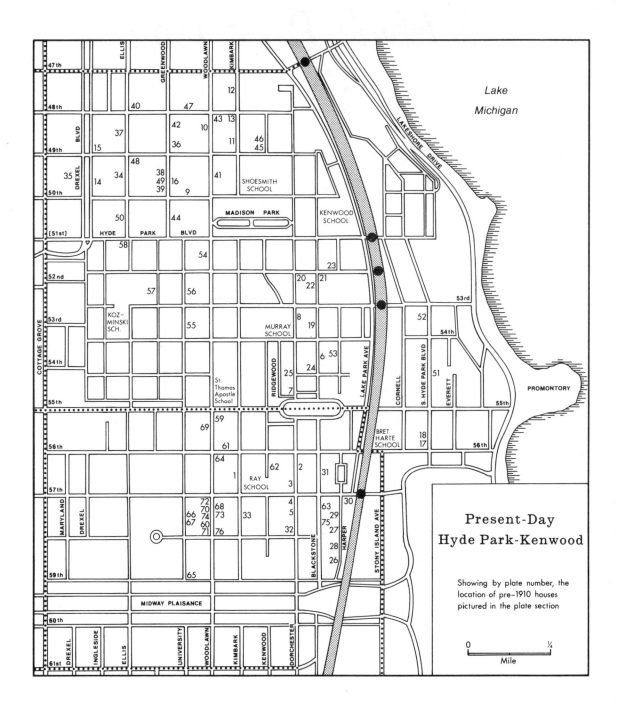

Present-Day Hyde Park–Kenwood

Showing by plate number, the location of pre-1910 houses pictured in the plate section

0   ¼
Mile

Lake Michigan

PROMONTORY

MIDWAY PLAISANCE

SHOESMITH SCHOOL

MADISON PARK

KENWOOD SCHOOL

KOZ-MINSKI SCH.

MURRAY SCHOOL

St. Thomas Apostle School

RAY SCHOOL

BRET HARTE SCHOOL

HYDE PARK BLVD

LAKESHORE DRIVE

LAKE PARK AVE

COTTAGE GROVE

ELLIS

GREENWOOD

WOODLAWN

KIMBARK

DREXEL

MARYLAND

DREXEL

BLACKSTONE

HARPER

STONY ISLAND AVE

CORNELL

S. HYDE PARK BLVD

EVERETT

RIDGEWOOD

INGLESIDE
ELLIS
UNIVERSITY
WOODLAWN
KIMBARK
KENWOOD
DORCHESTER

I

5630 Kimbark Ave.
Before 1868
(P. 14)

2, 3

Opposite page:
5607 Dorchester Ave.
C. 1870
(P. 14)

Right:
5642 Dorchester Ave.
Barn, c. 1869
(P. 14)

4

5704 Dorchester Ave.
William Hoyt, 1869
(P. 14)

5

5714 Dorchester Ave.
Charles Botsford, 1860
(P. 14)

6, 7, 8, 9

Right:
5417 Blackstone Ave.
Amanda Mick, c. 1868
(P. 15)

Opposite page:

(*above, left*)
5474 Dorchester Ave.
Before 1871
(P. 15)

(*above, right*)
5317 Dorchester Ave.
Henry C. Work, c. 1860
(P. 15)

(*below*)
1030 East 50th St.
Ezra S. Brainerd, 1867
(P. 15)

4812 Woodlawn Ave.
C. S. Bouton, 1873
(P. 38)

II, 12

Right:
4826–50 Kimbark Ave.
1880s
(P. 38)

Below:
4734 Kimbark Ave.
Reynolds Fisher,
before 1890
Patton & Fisher, archs.
(P. 39)

13, 14

Right:
4800 Kimbark Ave.
G. L. Miller, 1888
G. A. Garnsey, arch.
(P. 39)

Opposite page:
4941 Drexel Ave.
J. H. Nolan, 1887
Burnham & Root, archs.
(P. 40)

15

4845 Drexel Ave.
Martin Ryerson, 1887
Treat & Foltz, archs.
(P. 40)

16

4935 Greenwood Ave.
Edward A. Turner, 1888
Solon S. Beman, arch.
(P. 40)

17

5522 Hyde Park Blvd.
Anderson, 1889
George Maher, arch. (?)
(P. 40)

18

5518 Hyde Park Blvd.
W. B. Conkey, c. 1889
George Maher, arch.
(P. 40)

19, 20

Right:
5322–28 Blackstone Ave.
C. 1876
(P. 41)

Below:
5201–09 Dorchester Ave.
C. 1888
(P. 41)

5219 Blackstone Ave.
Myrtella Wilkins, 1889
(P. 41)

22, 23

Right:
5216 Blackstone Ave.
George Stoddard, 1885
(P. 41)

Below:
5146 Harper Ave.
W. C. Ott, 1884
(P. 41)

24, 25

Right:
5426–32 Blackstone Ave.
(P. 41)

Below:
5436–40 Dorchester Ave.
Frank I. Bennett, 1882
(P. 41)

26, 27

Opposite page:
5832–34 Harper Ave.
John A. Jackman, Jr., 1884
Solon S. Beman, arch.
(P. 42)

Right:
5752 Harper Ave.
Charles Bonner, 1889
W. W. Boyington, arch.
(P. 43)

28, 29

Right:
5810 Harper Ave.
William Waterman, 1884
H. F. Starbuck, arch.
(P. 43)

Opposite page:
5736 Harper Ave.
M. C. Armour, c. 1888
(P. 43)

30, 31, 32

Right:
5709 Harper Ave.
1509–17 E. 57th St.
J. Buckingham, 1889
(P. 43)

Below:
5621 Blackstone Ave.
W. C. Zimmerman, 1887
Flanders & Zimmerman,
archs.
(P. 43)

Opposite page:
5720–26 Dorchester Ave.
C. 1882
(P. 43)

5733 Kimbark Ave.
Before 1890
(P. 44)

4938–42 Ellis Ave.
C. A. Marshall, 1891
Wilson & Marshall,
archs.
(P. 76)

35, 36

Right:
4938 Drexel Ave.
J. A. McGill, 1890
Henry Ives Cobb, arch.
(P. 77)

Opposite page:
4857 Greenwood Ave.
John B. Lord, 1896
Charles Frost, arch.
(P. 77)

37

4848 Ellis Ave.
Gustavus Swift, 1898
Flanders & Zimmerman,
archs.
(P. 77)

38

4920 Greenwood Ave.
Enos M. Barton, 1901
Frost & Granger, archs.
(P. 77)

39, 40

Right:
4840 Greenwood Ave.
C. A. Goodyear, 1902
W. C. Zimmerman, arch.
(P. 77)

Opposite page:
1000 East 48th St.
William Fenton, 1902
Wilson & Marshall, archs.
(P. 77)

41

4929 Woodlawn
C. E. Scribner, 1906
Horatio Wilson, arch.
(P. 77)

42

4819 Greenwood Ave.
Joseph Schaffner, 1904
Holobird & Roche, archs.
(P. 78)

43, 44

Right:
4815 Woodlawn
T. E. Wilson, 1910
Howard Van Doren Shaw,
arch.
(P. 78)

Opposite page:
5017 Greenwood Ave.
H. Stillwell, 1905
Jarvis Hunt, arch.
(P. 78)

45, 46

Right:
4858 Kenwood Ave.
George Blossom, 1892
Frank Lloyd Wright, arch.
(P. 78)

Opposite page:
4852 Kenwood Ave.
Warren McArthur, 1892
Frank Lloyd Wright, arch.
(P. 78)

47, 48, 49

Right:
1120 East 48th St.
J. J. Wait, 1898
Dwight Perkins, arch.
(P. 79)

Opposite page (above):
4901 Ellis Ave.
Julius Rosenwald, 1903
Nimmons & Fellows, archs.
(P. 79)

(below)
4930 Greenwood Ave.
Ernest J. Magerstadt, 1908
George Maher, arch.
(P. 79)

50, 51

Opposite page:
5024 and 5030 Ellis Ave.
Apartment houses
E. Schoenfeld, Joseph
De Lee, 1909
George Maher, arch.
(P. 80)

Right:
5451–55 Hyde Park Blvd.
Phelps J. Lauten, 1907
Fromman & Jebson, archs.
(P. 80)

52, 53

Right:
5310–16, 5318–22 Hyde
Park Blvd.
Sherman T. Cooper, 1908
Andrew Sandegren, arch.
Sherman T. Cooper, 1904
Horatio Wilson, arch.
(P. 80)

Opposite page:
5416 Harper Ave.
O. M. Powers, 1892
Treat & Foltz, archs.
(P. 81)

5132 Woodlawn Ave.
Isidore Heller, 1897
Frank Lloyd Wright, arch.
(P. 81)

55

5317 University Ave.
Alice Tomlinson, 1904
Solon S. Beman, arch.
(P. 81)

56, 57

Right:
5235 University Ave.
H. W. Finch, 1904
James Gamble Rogers,
arch.
(P. 81)

Opposite page:
5200–08 Greenwood Ave.
S. E. Gross, 1903
J. C. Brompton, arch.
(P. 82)

58, 59

Right:
5100–16 Ellis Ave.
949–53 E. 51st St.
Apartment house
G. Freund, 1910
Horatio Wilson, arch.
(P. 82)

Opposite page:
5515 Woodlawn Ave.
Apartment house
F. I. Carpenter, before
1894
Pond & Pond, archs.
(P. 84)

60, 61

Right:
5730 Woodlawn Ave.
Bachelors' Club, 1896
Harvey L. Page, arch.
(P. 84)

Opposite page:
1222, 1226, 1228, 1234
E. 56th St.
Professors' houses, 1904
Mann, MacNeille, archs.
(P. 84)

62, 63

Opposite page:
5601–07 Kenwood Ave.
Professors' houses, 1905
Mann, MacNeille, &
Lindeberg, archs.
(P. 84)

Right:
5719–23 Blackstone Ave.
W. S. Whiton, 1896
Robert Spencer, arch.
(P. 84)

64, 65

Right:
1215–17 East 56th St.
5601–09 Woodlawn Ave.
Professors' houses, 1908
Tallmadge & Watson,
archs.
(P. 84)

Opposite page:
5855 University Ave.
William Rainey
Harper, 1894
Henry Ives Cobb, arch.
(P. 84)

66

5727 University Ave.
W. G. Hale, 1897
Hugh Garden, arch.
(P. 85)

67

5735 University Ave.
Robert Herrick, 1902
Hugh Garden, arch.
(P. 85)

5711 Woodlawn Ave.
Robert Wiles, 1901
Dwight Perkins, arch.
(P. 85)

69

5540 Woodlawn Ave.
Dr. E. Fletcher Ingalls,
1906
Holabird & Roche, archs.
(P. 85)

70

5720 Woodlawn Ave.
E. O. Jordan, 1898
Hartwell & Richardson,
archs.
(P. 85)

71

5740 Woodlawn Ave.
H. H. Donaldson, 1895
Patton & Fisher, archs.
(P. 85)

72, 73

Opposite page:
5706 Woodlawn Ave.
Edgar Goodspeed, 1906
Howard Van Doren Shaw,
arch.
(P. 86)

Right:
5715 Woodlawn Ave.
A. J. Mason, 1904
Howard Van Doren Shaw,
arch.
(P. 86)

74

5728 Woodlawn Ave.
Mrs. William Rainey
Harper, 1907
Howard Van Doren Shaw,
arch.
(P. 86)

5747 Blackstone Ave.
James W. Thompson, 1899
Pond & Pond, archs.
(P. 86)

5757 Woodlawn Ave.
Frederick Robie, 1909
Frank Lloyd Wright, arch.
(P. 86)

Appendix B
Checklist of Existing Dwellings

The date assigned to each of the buildings listed is the date when the first notice appeared. We can safely assume that barring bricklayers' strikes or changes in plans or architects, the house or apartment was built within six months after this time, some much sooner. The permit for the Vincent house, at 5737 University, for instance, was issued on June 9, 1897, and the notice states that the house will be ready for the roof on June 30. Much depended on the time of year the permit was issued or contracts let; if in January or February, work was not likely to commence until the ground had thawed.

For houses for which there is no permit, chiefly those put up before 1890, some may be dated from notices of architects' plans appearing in *Building Budget, Inland Architect,* or the *Chicago Tribune.* Other pre-1890 house have been dated from the first mention of the house in the *Hyde Park Herald* or the *Hyde Park News*— for rent, for sale, or as someone's residence. In the last instance the name of the resident was traced back in the *Lakeside Directory* or the *Blue Book* to the earliest date at which it appeared at that address.

Errors often occurred in the notices for permits, for contracts let, in the reports of architects' plans, and even in the assigning of an owner's name and address to a published photograph of a house. I have tried to correct these errors in names and their spellings and in street numbers, so far as possible, by checking the listings in the *Lakeside Directory.* Furthermore, over the years addresses changed as lots were divided. Thus, 4800 Woodlawn is now 4812, and 5731 Woodlawn has become 5729. If in checking a reference a discrepancy is found, it may be because such a correction was made.

Finally, it should be added that not all the dwellings erected before 1910 have been identified. Architects and builders did not always send in notices to professional journals and trade papers, nor did all builders obtain permits. There remain a number of mystery houses that look as if they belong to this period. Further work on them is indicated.

Key

b.	before
c.	about
pl.	plate
*	Multiple-family dwelling
AR	*Architectural Review*
BB	*Building Budget*
B	*Brickbuilder*
CN	*Construction News*
CP	City Permit
CR	County Recorder
C	Craig, James P. *A Holiday at Rosalie Villas*
D	Directory
Dr.	John Drury, *Old Chicago Houses*
E	*The Economist*
HABS	Historical American Buildings Survey
HPH	*Hyde Park Herald*
HPN	*Hyde Park News*
IA	*Inland Architect*
NW	*Northwestern Architect*
R	*Rascher's Atlas of Hyde Park,* 1890
RI	Resident informant
T	*Chicago Tribune*
UCW	*University of Chicago Weekly*
WA	*Western Architect*

NOTE: All numeral dates are given in the order *month/day/year* or *month/year*.

HYDE PARK
Everett Avenue

Date	Address	Owner	Occupation	Architect/Builder	Source
1910*	5478–84	William Doerr	real estate broker	Doerr & Doerr	CN/5/14/10
1910*	5514–22	William Doerr	real estate broker	Doerr & Doerr	CN/10/15/10
1909*	5524	David Hanson		Arthur Foster	CN/4/10/09

South Hyde Park Boulevard (East End Avenue)

Date	Address	Owner	Occupation	Architect/Builder	Source
1909*	5100	E. & J. P. Smith		Horatio R. Wilson	WA/5/13/pl.; CN/8/7/09
1892	5110	H. R. Hobart	pres., *Railway Age*		CP/9/21/92
1900	5222	John Stuart Coonley	manufacturer & rancher	Pond & Pond	B/11/03/pl.; CN/10/27/00
1908*	5310–22	Sherman T. Cooper	builder	Andrew Sandegren	CN/12/26/08
1909*	5324–30	Sherman T. Cooper	builder	Horatio R. Wilson	CN/10/30/09
1910*	5336			Sinclair M. Seator	CN/1/15/10
1900	5407	B. Witt		William H. Pruyn, Jr.	CN/8/29/08
1910*	5411–13	M. Anderson	"agent"	Andrew Sandegren	CN/4/23/10
1901	5421	Emily C. Weeks		George H. Borst	CN/7/20/01
1909*	5427–29	Harry F. Morris	sash & door mfr.	Doerr & Doerr	CN/11/6/09
1910*	5431–39	Harry F. & W. Morris	sash & door mfr.	David Robertson	CN/5/7/10
1902	5434	J. W. Clover	furniture retailer	C. F. Jobson	CN/6/14/02
1897	5441, 5445	Wheeler & Goldsmith		William H. Pruyn, Jr.	CN/6/16/97
1907	5454	Harriet Crandall	teacher	F. Baker	CN/6/22/07
1907*	5451–55	Philip J. Lauten	builder	Frommann & Jebson	CN/6/22/07
1902	5450	R. S. Thompson	attorney	Borst & Hetherington	CN/9/13/02
1910*	5457–59	Charles Anderson		Andrew Sandegren	CN/11/5/10
1908*	5463–65	Harry Morris	sash & door mfr.	Doerr & Doerr	CN/11/14/08
1906*	5474–80	Frank Gustafson	real estate developer	Andrew Sandegren	CN/4/21/06
1891	5482, 5484	D. Johnston & L. P. Perry		George Maher	E/6/13/91
1908*	5487–99	William P. Doerr	real estate broker	Doerr & Doerr	CN/4/4/08
1909*	5501–03	W. A. Worthington		H. W. Tomlinson	CN/4/11/09

Date	Address	Owner	Occupation	Architect/Builder	Source
1908*	5519	Charles R. Horrie	grocer	De Witt T. Kennard	CN/4/11/08
1888	5518	William B. Conkey	publisher	George Maher	T/9/21/88; NW/10/92/pl.
1888	5522	N. Anderson	"agent"	George Maher	T/9/21/88
1910*	5523–27	Charles Horrie		Charles W. Stevens	CN/10/1/10
1895	5533	Henry C. Thompson	"manager"	Howard Van Doren Shaw	E/2/9/95; IA/11/95/pl.

Cornell Avenue

Date	Address	Owner	Occupation	Architect/Builder	Source
1897	5124	Arthur B. Mulvey	real estate broker	Henry K. Holsman	CN/10/27/97; B/3/04
1898	5130	Arthur B. Mulvey	real estate broker	Brainerd & Holsman	IA/5/98
1897	5138–40	Arthur B. Mulvey	real estate broker	Brainerd & Holsman	CN/6/16/97
1896	5320	Hugh Daley	contractor	Arthur Foster	E/1/25/96
1896	5322	J. C. Daley		Arthur Foster	E/1/25/96
1909*	5323–29	Sherman T. Cooper	builder	L. M. Mitchell	CN/6/5/09
1907*	5413–15			Thomas McCall	CN/6/8/07
1907*	5417–19	G. Johnson		A. G. Lund	CN/6/15/07
1908*	5430	J. Frank McKinley	physician	Rapp & Rapp	CN/1/4/08
1908*	5539–43	C. L. Anderson	contractor	Rapp & Rapp	CN/11/21/08
1897	5434, 5436, 5438	Maria Bennett		Henry Bernritter	CN/11/17/97
1907*	5443–45	Henry F. Morris	sash & door mfr.	Doerr & Doerr	CN/12/14/07
1889	5505	John C. Fleming	steel mill exec.	R. G. Pentecost	T/9/22/89
1891	5517, 5519	Alex F. Shuman	real estate broker	George Maher?	T/9/6/91
1909*	5521	T. W. Gibbons		A. G. Lund	CN/11/28/08
1909*	5527–29	John W. Coutts		Thomas McCall	CN/11/7/08
1890	5533, 5535, 5537	Alex F. Shuman	real estate broker	George Maher?	IA/5/90
1908	5539	M. Anderson	"agent"	Anderson & Nelson	CP/11/4/08

Harper Avenue (Jefferson Avenue)

Date	Address	Owner	Occupation	Architect/Builder	Source
1891	5110, 5112, 5114	C. A. Kapp			CP/4/3/91

Date	Address	Owner	Occupation	Architect/Builder	Source
b. 1888	5135, 5137	Collie V. Mason			HPH/10/26/88
b. 1885	5146	W. C. Ott	lumber dealer		HPH/6/6/85
1895	5206	S. Carr			CP/6/11/95
1908*	5317–43	Henry Phipps	steel mill exec.	Jenney, Mundie & Jenson	CN/11/21/08
1890	5410	C. M. Oughton	physician	Minard L. Beers	T/1/27/90
1889	5411	L. A. Barstow			HPN/6/8/89
b. 1890	5415	L. A. Barstow			R
1892	5416	Orville M. Powers	prin. business college	Treat & Foltz	E/6/4/92
1905*	5427–33	John A. Carroll	attorney, real estate broker	Thomas McCall	CN/6/3/05

Harper Avenue (Rosalie Court)

Date	Address	Owner	Occupation	Architect/Builder	Source
1884	5708	J. C. Cook	physician	Solon S. Beman	IA/9/84
b. 1890	5711				R
b. 1890	5713				R
b. 1890	5715				R
b. 1890	5716				R
b. 1890	5719				R
b. 1890	5720				R
b. 1890	5721				R
b. 1890	5724				R
b. 1890	5725				R
1888	5728	C. G. Field	druggist		HPH/9/14/88
b. 1890	5729				R
b. 1890	5731				R
1884	5732	Frederick Reynolds	accountant	Solon S. Beman	IA/9/84
b. 1890	5735				R
b. 1888	5736	M. C. Armour	iron merchant		HPH/5/18/88
1888	5739	Waddell			Craig
1885	5740	H. T. Chase	real estate broker		D 1885
1888	5743	Waddell			Craig

Date	Address	Owner	Occupation	Architect/Builder	Source
1886	5744	E. W. Heath	manufacturer	W. I. Beman	BB/4/86
1888	5745	W. C. Hobbs			HPH/1/13/88
b. 1890	5749				R
1885	5751	Irving K. Pond	architect	Irving K. Pond	IA/5/85
1889	5752	Charles Bonner	brick mfr.	William W. Boyington	IA/4/89
1885	5755	Irving K. Pond	architect	Irving K. Pond	IA/6/85
b. 1890	5756				R
1884	5759	Frederick Reynolds		Solon S. Beman	IA/9/84
1894	5762	Emma Over		Stiles & Stone	IA/5/94
b. 1890	5763				R
b. 1890	5800				R
b. 1890	5801				R
b. 1890	5803				R
b. 1890	5804				R
b. 1890	5806				R
b. 1890	5807				R
1888	5809	R. L. Morley	"assistant manager"	E. Clarke Johnson	BB/4/88
1884	5810	William Waterman		Henry F. Starbuck	IA/10/84
b. 1890	5812				R
b. 1890	5816				R
b. 1890	5822				R
1884	5824	John A. Jackman, Jr.	manager, Pullman	Solon S. Beman	IA/9/84
1884	5832	John A. Jackman, Jr.	manager, Pullman	Solon S. Beman	IA/9/84
1884	5834	John A. Jackman, Jr.	manager, Pullman	Solon S. Beman	IA/9/84
b. 1890	5838				R
1902*	5842–44	C. D. Armstrong	builder	Bishop & Co.	CN/5/24/02

Blackstone Avenue (Washington Avenue)

Date	Address	Owner	Occupation	Architect/Builder	Source
1893	5114–16	W. Fish			D
1892	5142	H. C. Allen	physician	Beman & Parmentier	NW/10/92

Date	Address	Owner	Occupation	Architect/Builder	Source
1903*	5201–03; 5207–09	W. P. Doerr	real estate broker	Doerr & Doerr	CN/10/17/03
1889	5211–21	Myrtella Wilkins			T/3/31/89
1886	5210	Fred G. Perry		William Clay	BB/6/86
1885	5216	George Stoddard	businessman (wholesale furniture)		RI
b. 1890	5314				R
1890	5318	David Quigg	attorney	Minard L. Beers	HPH/6/27/90
c. 1875	5322–28	Walter S. Johnson	physician		CR
b. 1890	5408				R
c. 1875	5410	Albert Veeder	attorney		CR
b. 1890	5412				R
b. 1890	5413				R
c. 1868	5417	Amanda Mick			CR
1887	5418–20	Della Philips			HPH/12/30/87
b. 1890	5422				R
b. 1890	5423				R
1888	5424				T/1/15/88
b. 1890	5425				R
b. 1890	5426				R
1895	5427, 5429	J. J. Miller	law printer	H. Flower	IA/9/95
b. 1890	5428				R
1888	5430	C. W. Mick	commercial traveler		HPH/8/3/88
b. 1890	5432				R
b. 1890	5434				R
1897	5530, 5532, 5534, 5536, 5538	Anna Root		Henry Bernritter	CN/11/10/97
1904*	5533–35	Sarah Brown		S. M. Seator	CN/5/14/04
1891	5545	Herman J. Hall	trader, Board of Trade	Frank B. Abbott	IA/11/91; NW/8/92/pl.
b. 1890	5547				R
1902*	5553–55	M. R. Potter	attorney	Thomas McCall	CN/5/3/02
1909*	5557–59			T. McCall	CN/7/3/09

Date	Address	Owner	Occupation	Architect/Builder	Source
b. 1890	5610				R
1886	5611	William Carbys Zimmerman	architect	Flanders & Zimmerman	CR
b. 1890	5620				R
1886	5621	William Carbys Zimmerman	architect	Flanders & Zimmerman	IA/10/86/pl.
1898	5626, 5628, 5630, 5632, 5634, 5636, 5638	Lucy Norton		John Stone	CN/10/19/98
b. 1890	5639				R
1906*	5647–49	Arthur Foster	architect	Arthur Foster	CN/10/3/06
1905*	5701–07	G. Fred Rush	attorney	C. M. Almquist	CN/11/4/05
1903*	5715	L. K. Whiton	broker	E. M. Newman	CN/11/28/03
1897	5717	W. S. Whiton	attorney	Henry Bernritter	CN/6/30/97
1896	5719, 5721, 5723	L. K. Whiton	broker	Robert Spencer	IA/12/96; B/3/04/pl.
b. 1887	5725	Fred K. Root	supt. special assessments		HPH/10/7/87
1892	5729, 5731	Henry V. Freeman	attorney	Beers, Clay, & Dutton	E/6/25/92
1888	5736, 5738	Henry H. Belfield	teacher	Cole & Dahlgren	T/11/11/88
1898	5733, 5735, 5737	Henry V. Freeman	attorney	C. M. Almquist	CN/11/23/98
b. 1890	5739				R
1894	5743, 5745	I. A. Sleeper	attorney		CP/8/6/94
b. 1890	5744				R
1899	5747	James W. Thompson	professor	Pond & Pond	IA/11/00/pl; CP/5/19/99; B/8/00/pl.
1899	5757, 5759	Katherine Rush		Nimmons & Fellows	CN/7/26/99
b. 1890	5761				R
1897	5801, 5803, 5805, 5807	Howard Sunderland	clerk, Armour	Henry Bernritter	CN/12/29/97
b. 1890	5809				R

Date	Address	Owner	Occupation	Architect/Builder	Source
b. 1890	5813				R
1909*	5825	Fred Bode	wholesale milliner	Marshall & Fox	CN/6/12/09
b. 1890	5827				R
1888	5831	Cora Riedle			HPH/4/27/88
1887	5837	Frank Riedle	real estate broker		D

Dorchester Avenue (Madison Avenue)

Date	Address	Owner	Occupation	Architect/Builder	Source
1893	5112	Wheeler & Goldsmith			CP/6/1/93
1895	5117, 5119	Wheeler & Goldsmith		Pond & Pond	E/4/20/95; IA/11/95/pl.
1895	5121, 5123, 5125, 5129, 5131	W. H. Moore		C. M. Palmer	E/11/2/95
1895	5137	C. H. Binney			CP/3/90/95
b. 1890	5201, 5203, 5205, 5207, 5209				R
1904*	5213–15	J. Schmitt		Doerr & Doerr	CN/4/9/04
1902*	5216–18	W. L. de Beck		Doerr & Doerr	CN/4/26/02
b. 1887	5217, 5219				T/8/14/87
1902*	5223–25	J. W. Eastland		R. S. Smith	CN/12/13/02
1904*	5227–29	C. T. Hallgren		Andrew Sandegren	CN/11/19/04
1860	5317	Henry C. Work	printer & songwriter		Dr.
1888	5319	Quinn	police magistrate		T/1/13/89
b. 1890	5321				R
c. 1868	5325	W. Ottaway			CR
1892	5330	George Wessel	merchant		CP/1/25/92
1909*	5400–02			Thomas McCall	CN/7/3/09
1889	5401, 5403, 5405				HPH/2/22/89
b. 1890	5406				R
c. 1878	5407	E. R. Williams			CR
b. 1890	5409				R
b. 1890	5410				R

Date	Address	Owner	Occupation	Architect/Builder	Source
b. 1890	5412				R
1892	5413	H. W. Wolesley	attorney		CP/4/13/92
b. 1890	5420				R
b. 1890	5422				R
1888	5430–32	A. J. Sinclair			HPH/11/9/88
1882	5436	Frank I. Bennett	attorney		T/2/18/82
1882	5438	Frank I. Bennett	attorney		T/2/18/82
1882	5440	Frank I. Bennett	attorney		T/2/18/82
1882	5442	Frank I. Bennett	attorney		T/2/18/82
b. 1890	5444				R
b. 1890	5445				R
1892	5446	H. D. Hess	milk dealer		CP/6/25/92
b. 1890	5448				R
b. 1890	5454				R
b. 1890	5462				R
b. 1890	5466				R
b. 1890	5468				R
b. 1890	5470				R
b. 1890	5472				R
b. 1890	5474				R
b. 1890	5476				R
1904*	5530	N. Johnson		A. G. Lund	CN/4/23/04
b. 1890	5532				R
1894	5533, 5535, 5537, 5539, 5541, 5543, 5545	Fred K. Root	music dealer	Fraenkel & Schmidt	E/12/94
1887	5542, 5546	Silas M. Moore	real estate broker	Silas M. Moore	T/10/15/87
1892	5601, 5603			Beers, Clay & Dutton	T/6/12/92
1883	5605	Leslie Lewis	supt. schools		D
b. 1871	5609	Thomas A. Banning	attorney		RI
1901*	5613–29	J. C. Cochran		L. M. Mitchell	CN/6/22/01
b. 1890	5614				R
1906*	5624–26	A. Stewart	sash & door mfr.	W. L. Klewer	CN/4/7/06

Date	Address	Owner	Occupation	Architect/Builder	Source
1906*	5625–29			W. L. Klewer	CN/3/17/06
1909*	5631–37			Thomas McCall	CN/4/26/09
1906	5638	Stephen Mather	mgr. Sterling Borax Co., 1st director Nat'l. Parks		RI
c. 1870	5642				RI
1869	5704	William H. Hoyt	real estate broker		RI; Dr
1887	5708–10	Marshall D. Wilbur			RI
1860	5714	Charles Botsford			Dr
1903*	5716–18	G. Low		Thomas McCall	CN/6/6/03
b. 1882	5722, 5724, 5726, 5728	Walter Nelson	real estate developer, contractor		T/3/5/82
1888	5729				HPH/8/3/88
b. 1890	5731				R
1887	5735				HPH/11/25/87
1888	5737				HPH/6/1/88
1886	5743, 5745, 5747, 5749	Walter Nelson	real estate developer, contractor	H. F. Dean	HPH/4/17/86
b. 1890	5751, 5753, 5755, 5759, 5761				R

Kenwood Avenue (Hibbard Street)

Date	Address	Owner	Occupation	Architect/Builder	Source
b. 1890	5111				R
1888	5201, 5203, 5205, 5207, 5209	Charles H. Root		Cole & Dahlgren	HPN/11/10/88
b. 1890	5206				R
1892	5210	George Hoyt	dry goods merchant	Arthur W. Cole	IA/6/92
b. 1890	5211				R
b. 1890	5213				R
b. 1890	5214				R
b. 1890	5215				R
1889	5222	W. I. Beman	architect	W. I. Beman	HPN/2/2/89
1889	5228	W. I. Beman	architect	W. I. Beman	HPN/2/2/89
1909*	5237–45	Collins & Morris	builders	Henry Newhouse	CN/1/30/09

	Date	Address	Owner	Occupation	Architect/Builder	Source
	b. 1890	5455				R
	b. 1890	5457–5459				R

Kenwood Avenue
(Monroe Avenue)

	Date	Address	Owner	Occupation	Architect/Builder	Source
	b. 1890	5538				R
	b. 1890	5540				R
	b. 1890	5543				R
	b. 1890	5544				R
	b. 1890	5546				R
	b. 1890	5548				R
	b. 1890	5552				R
	b. 1890	5553				R
	b. 1890	5554				R
	b. 1890	5555				R
	b. 1890	5557				R
	1903	5603	E. B. Hutchinson	professor	Mann, MacNeille, Lindeberg	IA/91/05/pl.; CN/10/24/03
	1903	5607	Alexander Smith	professor	Mann, MacNeille, Lindeberg	IA/91/05/pl.; CN/10/24/03
	1903	5609	Eliakim H. Moore	professor	Mann, MacNeille, Lindeberg	IA/91/05/pl.; CN/10/24/03
	1903	5611	George Hendrikson	professor	Mann, MacNeille, Lindeberg	IA/91/05/pl.; CN/10/24/03
	1903	5615	Edward T. Lee	dean, John Marshall Law School	Mann, MacNeille, Lindeberg	IA/91/05/pl.; CN/10/24/03
	b. 1890	5621				R
	b. 1890	5625				R
	b. 1890	5629				R
	1900*	5704	J. Lally		Thomas McCall	CP/7/3/10
	1897*	5701–09	Walter Nelson	real estate developer, contractor	John Stone	IA/10/97; CN/1/5/98/pl.
	b. 1890	5708				R
	1892	5723, 5725, 5727, 5729, 5735, 5737	Walter Nelson	real estate broker	Stiles & Stone	CP/12/2/92
	1909*	5714–24	John B. Jackson	minister	Argyle Robinson	CN/4/17/09

Date	Address	Owner	Occupation	Architect/Builder	Source
b. 1890	5726	John B. Jackson	minister		R; RI
1889	5730	William R. Patterson	supt.	Treat & Foltz	T/8/25/89
1892	5732	Nicholas Hunt	police chief	Stiles & Stone	T/10/30/92
1894*	5742, 5744	Nicholas Hunt	police chief	Stiles & Stone	E/10/27/94
1910*	5756–58	F. E. Livingood	salesman	Thomas McCall	CN/10/1/10
1901	5801	Frank R. Lillie	professor	Pond & Pond	IA/2/03/pl.; CN/10/26/01
1895	5811	William Wilder	physician	L. Green	RI; IA/11/95

Kimbark Avenue (Jackson Avenue)

Date	Address	Owner	Occupation	Architect/Builder	Source
1893	5107–09	M. A. Vinal			CP/8/29/93
1906*	5117–19	M. Anderson		A. G. Lund	CN/6/23/06
1889	5120	C. S. Dennis	attorney	Treat & Foltz	T/8/25/89
1890	5121	C. E. Conover			CP/8/13/90
1889	5200, 5202	Atwood Vane	real estate broker	Beman & Parmentier	HPN/2/2/89
b. 1890	5206				R
b. 1890	5208				R
b. 1890	5211, 5213, 5214, 5215				R
1895	5400, 5402, 5404, 5406, 5408, 5410, 5412	Jacob Franks	broker		CP/7/29/95
b. 1890	5420				R
b. 1890	5446				R
1908*	5528	Eliza Shaw		W. M. Walter	CN/2/2/08
1908*	5536	R. Bobb	grocer	T. McCall	CN/1/4/08
1904	5558	Francis Shepardson	professor	Mann, MacNeille	IA/11/06/pl.; CN/2/13/04
1909*	5616–18	E. Metzger		O. A. Kupfer	CN/7/17/09
b. 1868	5630				RI
1906*	5642	E. Washburn		Thomas McCall	CN/7/21/06
1893	5722	D. H. Stapp	lawyer	J. E. O. Pridmore	E/2/25/93
1902	5724	Wilbur S. Jackman	professor	Howard Van Doren Shaw	CN/10/18/02

Date	Address	Owner	Occupation	Architect/Builder	Source
c. 1879	5727	Johnson	carpenter		RI
b. 1890	5729				R
1907	5730	W. S. Jackman		Howard Van Doren Shaw	B/5/10/pl. 70; CN/6/15/07
b. 1890	5733				R
1891	5734	V. L. Cunningham	cashier		CP/3/25/91
b. 1890	5737				R
b. 1890	5739				R
1905	5740	F. G. Wright	paper mfr.	John Stone	CN/7/29/05
b. 1890	5741				R
b. 1890	5743				R
1907	5744	Charles Eaton	attorney	Howard Van Doren Shaw	B/5/10/pl. 68; CN/3/16/07
1908	5757	William G. Hale	professor	Argyle Robinson	CN/5/2/08

Ridgewood Court (Tompkins Place)

Date	Address	Owner	Occupation	Architect/Builder	Source
b. 1890	5405, 5411, 5413, 5419, 5421, 5423, 5427, 5429, 5443, 5445, 5447, 5455, 5456, 5458, 5465, 5467, 5470, 5475, 5476, 5477, 5481				R
1882	5437-39–41-43			Frank I. Bennett	T/2/18/82

Woodlawn Avenue (Van Buren)

Date	Address	Owner	Occupation	Architect/Builder	Source
1891	5116	M. R. Donnelly			CP/2/2/91
1909	5127	S. G. Lowden		W. F. Shattuck	CN/6/5/09
1897	5132	Isadore Heller	packer	Frank Lloyd Wright	B/9/03/pl.; HABS
b. 1890	5134				R
1908*	5316–18	M. Olson		Turnquist Bros.	CP/1/10/08
1899*	5401–03	W. McGuire		Anderson & Johnson	CP/5/15/99
1909*	5431–37			Bishop & Co.	CN/10/2/09
b. 1890	5480				R
1894*	5515	James Miller		Pond & Pond	CP/6/17/92; IA/1/94/pl.; B/11/03
1908	5521	H. Vanderploeg	attorney	W. Banfield	CN/10/3/08

Date	Address	Owner	Occupation	Architect/Builder	Source
1905	5525	Ernest D. Burton	professor	Thomas McCall	CN/9/16/05
1903	5528	George Hamlin	singer	James Gamble Rogers	CN/5/30/03
1899	5533	Frederick Ives Carpenter	professor	Pond & Pond	IA/6/99/pl.
1899	5537	George M. Eckels	attorney	Henry Holsman	CN/10/25/99
1905	5539–41	B. A. Streich	bookkeeper	Howard Van Doren Shaw	CN/2/18/05
1905	5540	E. Fletcher Ingalls	physician	Holabird & Roche	CN/5/27/05
1898	5542	George Crilly	attorney	William M. Crilly	CP/10/27/98
1892	5554	Theodore F. Rice	paper mfr.	Mifflin E. Bell	IA/5/92
1897	5548	I. K. Hamilton		J. M. Van Osdel	IA/2/97
1907	5605	Robert Millikan	professor	Tallmadge & Watson	CN/4/13/07
1907	5609	Andrew McLaughlin	professor	Tallmadge & Watson	CN/4/13/07
1909	5615	Bertram W. Sippy	physician	Howard Van Doren Shaw	CN/6/19/09
1909	5625	Charles Miller	lumber merchant	Pond & Pond	CN/10/30/09
1896	5630	William C. Wilkinson	professor	Henry Ives Cobb	IA/12/96
1909	5633	Roy O. West	attorney	William Carbys Zimmerman	CN/2/13/09
1905	5637	Lucius Teter	banker	Holabird & Roche	CN/10/14/05
1905	5641	Charles W. Hoff	builder	Bishop & Co.	CN/11/4/05
1907	5645	Frank H. Connor	cattle broker	Charles W. Hoff	CP/4/5/07
1903	5649	Andrew J. Herschl	attorney	H. S. Jaffray	CN/12/5/03
1902	5659	James Rankin	grain & provisions merchant	Borst & Hetherington	CN/9/13/02
1906	5706	Edgar Goodspeed	professor	Howard Van Doren Shaw	CN/5/26/06
1909	5707	W. B. Wolff	manufacturer	William Carbys Zimmerman	CN/2/13/09
1901	5710	George Middendorf	professor	Robert Rae	CN/10/12/01
1901	5711	Russell Wiles	attorney	Dwight Perkins	B/9/03/pl.; CN/5/11/01

Date	Address	Owner	Occupation	Architect/Builder	Source
1905	5714	Floyd R. Mechem	professor	Mann, MacNeille	CN/4/15/05
1904	5715	Arthur J. Mason	engineer	Howard Van Doren Shaw	B/8/06/pl.; CN/1/30/04
1897	5720	Edwin O. Jordan	physician	Hartwell, Richardson & Driver (Myron Hunt)	CN/9/29/97; IA/1/98; pl.
1900	5725	George C. Howland	professor	Rapp and Rapp	CN/7/7/00
1901	5729	John A. Roche	ex-mayor of Chicago	Rapp and Rapp	CN/12/1/00; IA/3/02/pl.
1906	5728	Mrs. W. R. Harper		Howard Van Doren Shaw	CN/3/10/06
1896	5730	Joseph Iddings, Frank Tarbell, Ernst Freund	professors	Harvey L. Page	E/3/14/96
1895	5736	Shailer Mathews	professor		UCW/4/11/95
1895	5740	Henry H. Donaldson	professor	Patton & Fisher	E/4/13/95
1896	5750	Albert H. Tolman	professor		UCW/12/17/96
1909	5757	Fred Robie	engineer	Frank Lloyd Wright	CN/3/20/09; HABS

University Avenue (Lexington Avenue)

Date	Address	Owner	Occupation	Architect/Builder	Source
1895	5130	E. E. Chandler	"department manager"	Treat & Foltz	E/11/23/95
1893	5137, 5139	M. B. Cummings	plumber		CP/11/13/93
1909	5206	H. F. Kellogg	engineer	Henry Webster Tomlinson	CN/8/14/09
1902	5211	William Perrin	mfr. packers' machinery	W. J. Brinkman	CN/3/22/02
1894	5217	J. M. Smith			CP/9/18/94
1904	5235	Homer N. Finch	coal merchant	James Gamble Rogers	IA/4/05/pl.; CN/7/9/04
1891	5247	Robert G. Smith	salesman	Beers, Clay & Dutton	E/4/25/91; IA/4/91
1910	5301			Arthur Foster	CN/10/29/10
1894	5307	George P. Barton	attorney		CP/6/14/94

Date	Address	Owner	Occupation	Architect/Builder	Source
1904	5310	J. Kipley		E. A. Blondin	CN/10/15/04
1906	5314	Charles Antoine	merchant	Sidney Lovell	CN/6/2/06
1904	5317	J. A. Tomlinson	insurance	Solon S. Beman	CN/9/24/04
1906	5321	Kate Miller		Theodore Duesing	CN/5/19/06
1907	5327	J. H. McNamara	manufacturer	Borst & Hetherington	CN/4/20/07
1900	5330	Mary A. Hearn		Doerr & Doerr	CN/7/14/00
1904	5400, 5402, 5404, 5406	S. M. Sargent		S. M. Eichberg	CN/3/12/04
1901	5416–18	Thomas Glenn	contractor	C. Schleyer	CP/7/15/01
1904	5533	Oskar Bolza	professor	Howard Van Doren Shaw	CN/6/4/04
1906	5541	Theodore G. Soares	professor	Thomas McCall	CN/7/21/06
1909	5545	Theodore G. Soares	professor	Sinclair M. Seator	CN/4/24/09
1897	5629	William D. MacClintock	professor	Arthur Maher	CP/6/30/97
1891	5635	N. I. Rubinkam	professor	E. Born	CP/3/30/97
1897	5727	William Gardner Hale	professor	Hugh M. Garden	B/11/03/pl.; IA/6/98/pl.; CN/8/18/97
1901	5733	Carl D. Buck	professor	Henry K. Holsman	B/11/03/pl.; CN/2/23/01
1901	5735	Robert Herrick	professor	Hugh Garden	B/11/03/pl.; IA/2/02/pl.
1897	5737	George Vincent	professor	Howard Van Doren Shaw	CN/6/9/97
1894	5855	William Rainey Harper	president, U. of Chicago	Henry Ives Cobb	IA/6/94; UCW/4/25/95/pl.

Greenwood Avenue

Date	Address	Owner	Occupation	Architect/Builder	Source
1903	5200–44	Samuel E. Gross	real estate broker		
		Charles Counselman	packer	J. C. Brompton	CN/5/2/03
1903	5309	C. Riborg Mann	professor	Mann, MacNeille	CN/10/24/03; IA/6/05/pl.
1903	5315	Edward Capps	physician	Mann, MacNeille	CN/10/24/03; IA/6/05/pl.

Date	Address	Owner	Occupation	Architect/Builder	Source
1903	5317	George Shambaugh	physician	Mann, MacNeille	CN/10/24/03; IA/6/05/pl.
1903	5321	Lester Bartlett	business mgr. *Journal*	Mann, MacNeille	CN/10/24/03; IA/6/05/pl.
b. 1890	5318				R
b. 1890	5329				R
b. 1890	5331				R
1902	5401–03–05	T. M. Glenn	contractor	C. Schleyer	CP/11/3/02
1902	5407	A. F. Wheeler		Arthur W. Cole	CN/12/27/02
1898	5411	E. E. Hill	teacher	Arthur W. Cole	IA/2/98
1898	5413	A. W. Cole	architect	Arthur W. Cole	IA/2/98
1902	5414	J. Meyers		N. McMillan	CP/4/16/02
1901	5417–19–21–23	T. M. Glenn	contractor	C. Schleyer	CP/11/1/01
b. 1890	5474				R
b. 1890	5478				R

Ellis Avenue

Date	Address	Owner	Occupation	Architect/Builder	Source
1910*	5100–16	Gustav Freund	packer	Horatio Wilson	CN/10/15/10
1909*	5121	J. Copeland		Harper Bros.	CP/12/7/09
1910*	5125	A. Harper		Henry Newhouse	CN/11/5/10
1909	5130	C. T. Zohringer		C. Schleyer	CP/10/29/09
1903	5323–25	J. A. Larson		Anderson & Winblau	CP/7/27/03
1904	5327, 5329	J. A. Larson		A. G. Lund	CN/1/30/04
1905	5423–47	Murray Wolbach	real estate broker	L. M. Mitchell	CN/1/14/05
1899	5481–83–85	W. H. Sweeney		J. Owens	CP/1/5/99

Drexel Avenue (Grove Avenue)

Date	Address	Owner	Occupation	Architect/Builder	Source
1907	5356	M. Raftree	builder	P. Hale	CN/4/27/07
b. 1890	5459				R
b. 1890	5467				R
b. 1890	5469				R
b. 1890	5471				R

	Date	Address	Owner	Occupation	Architect/Builder	Source
	b. 1890	5473				R
	b. 1890	5475				R
	b. 1890	5610				R
	b. 1890	5623				R
	b. 1890	5626				R
	b. 1890	5630				R
	1900*	5659–61	Keith Bros.		L. E. Stanhope	CN/12/29/00
	1908*	5728–30	E. Winter		Henry Newhouse	CN/10/31/08
East Hyde Park Boulevard (East 51st Street; Laurel Street)	1910*	931–49			William Pruyn, Jr.	CN/10/29/10
	1910*	949–53	Gustav Freund	packer	Horatio Wilson	CN/10/15/10
	1889	1321, 1325, 1327	W. I. Beman	architect	W. I. Beman	HPN/9/14/89
	1909*	1615–35	J. P. & E. Smith		Horatio Wilson	CN/8/7/09
East 52nd Street (Grove Street)	1909*	941–45	E. F. Henshaw		John Stone	CN/11/13/09
	1890	1314, 1316	W. Dykeman			CP/11/10/90
	b. 1890	1351				R
	b. 1890	1361	A. S. Terry			R
	c. 1895	1368	A. S. Terry	steel mill exec.	F. W. Kirkpatrick	D; IA/2/02/pl.
	c. 1895	1372	R. P. Lamont			
East 54th Street (Chestnut Street)	1894	1160, 1162	E. Goehst	plumber		CP/8/8/94
	1895	1164	E. Goehst	plumber		CP/12/5/95
East 54th Place	b. 1890	1412				R
	b. 1890	1416				R
	b. 1890	1418				R
	b. 1890	1452				R
East 55th Street (Elm Street)	1909*	1716–26	C. A. Carlson		Andrew Sandegren	CN/11/13/09
East 56th Street (Ash Street)	b. 1890	1320				R

128

Date	Address	Owner	Occupation	Architect/Builder	Source
1903	1363	Theodore L. Neff	professor	Mann, MacNeille, Lindeberg	IA/91/05/pl.; CN/10/24/03
b. 1890	1360				R
1903	1357	Charles R. Barnes	professor	Mann, MacNeille, Lindeberg	IA/91/05/pl.; CN/10/24/03
1903	1351	Andrew Allen	professor	Mann, MacNeille, Lindeberg	IA/91/05/pl.; CN/10/24/03
b. 1890	1322				R
1904	1232	K. B. Miller	engineer	Mann, MacNeille	IA/11/06/pl.; CN/2/13/04
1904	1228	Francis Blackburn	professor	Mann, MacNeille	IA/11/06/pl.; CN/2/13/04
1904	1224	Mrs. Paul Kern	teacher	Mann, MacNeille	IA/11/06/pl.; CN/2/13/04
1904	1222	Frank J. Miller	professor	Mann, MacNeille	IA/11/06/pl.; CN/2/13/04
1904	1220	Herbert L. Willett	professor	Mann, MacNeille	IA/11/06/pl.; CN/2/13/04
1907	1215	Andrew Allen	engineer	Tallmadge & Watson	CN/4/13/07
1907	1201	Clarke B. Whittier	professor	Tallmadge & Watson	CN/4/13/07
1902*	1154–56	I. N. Rubinkam	professor	A. W. Buckley	CN/11/22/02

East 57th Street (Willow Street)

Date	Address	Owner	Occupation	Architect/Builder	Source
1889*	(5709 Harper) 1509–17	J. Buckingham			T/6/16/89
1908*	1413–15	G. Morrison	builder	Arthur Foster	CN/5/2/08
1897*	1355–57–59–61	Walter Nelson	real estate broker	John Stone	IA/10/97; CN/1/5/98/pl.
1887	1220	O. M. Wells & Co.	real estate brokers		T/1/2/87
1887	1224	O. M. Wells & Co.	real estate brokers		T/1/2/87
1910*	1227–29			John Stone	CN/4/16/10
1887	1232	O. M. Wells & Co.	real estate brokers		T/1/2/87
1887	1236	O. M. Wells & Co.	real estate brokers		T/1/2/87

East 58th Street (Cedar Street)

Date	Address	Owner	Occupation	Architect/Builder	Source
1907*	1356–60			Thomas McCall	CN/4/20/07

Date	Address	Owner	Occupation	Architect/Builder	Source
1908	1308	James Parker Hall	professor	Argyle Robinson	CN/5/2/08

KENWOOD
Blackstone Avenue (Washington Avenue)

Date	Address	Owner	Occupation	Architect/Builder	Source
b. 1890	4916				R
1891	5000, 5002, 5004			W. I. Beman	CP/11/7/91
1897	5008	H. A. Larmine		O. W. Marble	CN/6/2/97
1902*	5014–20	K. B. Williams		I. E. Stanhope	CN/3/22/02
1891	5026, 5028, 5030, 5032, 5034, 5036, 5038	Taylor, Allen & Co.		O. W. Marble	IA/6/91; CP/6/15/91
b. 1890	5040				R
1906*	5046–56	J. Cormack		Thomas McCall	CN/10/6/06

Dorchester Avenue (Madison Street)

Date	Address	Owner	Occupation	Architect/Builder	Source
1908	4800–10	Charles W. Hoff	real estate broker	Bishop & Co.	CN/1/25/08
1906*	4816–28	Claus Carlson	builder	A. Sandegren	CN/8/25/06
1903	4836	Robert J. McLaughlin		L. D. Quackenboss	CN/4/4/03
1897	4858	Archibald Church	physician	Handy & Cady	IA/12/97; CN/11/10/97
1888	4913	Edward H. Turner	dry goods dealer	William Craig	RI
1892	4919	Horatio L. Wait	attorney		CP/12/8/92
1890	4921	A. H. Trotter	salesman	Frederick W. Perkins	BB/9/90
b. 1890	4927				R
1909*	4933	Henry Peterson		Thomas McCall	CN/2/27/09
1904*	5001–07	Hood & Tullgren	builders	S. M. Seator	CN/5/21/04
1901*	5008–14	William Doerr	real estate broker	Doerr & Doerr	CN/12/28/01
b. 1890	5015				R
1891	5027, 5029, 5031, 5035	Batchen Bros.		C. S. Johnson	E/9/12/91

Kenwood Avenue

Date	Address	Owner	Occupation	Architect/Builder	Source
1888	4800	Joseph R. Putnam	real estate broker		HPN/8/11/88
1888	4801	H. S. Coulter		Treat & Foltz	HPN/12/8/88
1905	4809	Robert Book, Jr.		J. Lemasney	CP/11/19/05

Date	Address	Owner	Occupation	Architect/Builder	Source
1890	4810	Kate B. Parish		Henry H. Sprague	IA/7/90/pl.
1889	4815	Joseph R. Putnam	real estate broker		HPN/6/8/89
1899	4816	E. J. Preston		A. W. Buckley	CN/10/18/99
1899	4820	Gurnee Fellows	physician	George C. Nimmons	CP/7/12/99
b. 1890	4822				R
1904	4823	Platt G. Gibbs	music dealer	Nimmons & Fellows	CN/10/1/04
1894	4827	H. R. Tenney	attorney	William Craig	CP/3/20/94
1896	4828	E. D. Kimball	iron	Diven & White	E/3/28/96
1892	4830	C. E. Matthews	gas machine mfr.	Flanders & Zimmerman	T/4/17/92
1891	4831	H. Ludington			CP/5/21/91
1894	4837	C. M. Ludington			CP/2/15/94
1902	4842	Charles F. Harding	attorney	Handy & Cady	CN/3/8/02
1901	4845	W. V. B. Ames	physician	J. Rodatz	CP/10/26/01
1901	4846	Ralph D. Farwell	asst. secy' Oak-woods cemetery ass.	R. G. Dwen	CN/6/8/01
1905	4849	Harry H. Waterman	architect	Harry H. Waterman	CN/4/8/05
1898	4851–53	E. G. Chase	broker	George C. Nimmons	CN/11/30/98
1892	4852	Warren McArthur	manufacturer	Frank Lloyd Wright	E/5/21/92
1892	4858	George Blossom	insurance exec.	Frank Lloyd Wright	E/5/21/92

Kimbark Avenue

Date	Address	Owner	Occupation	Architect/Builder	Source
b. 1890	4730				R
1890	4734	Reynolds Fisher	architect	Patton & Fisher	IA/7/90/pl.
b. 1890	4737				R
1888	4740	Joseph H. Howard	lumber merchant		HPN/8/11/88
b. 1890	4744				R
1886	4747	William R. Page		Jenney and Otis	HPN/12/4/86; BB/11/86;

Date	Address	Owner	Occupation	Architect/Builder	Source
1884	4752	Walter G. Coolidge	pres. Chicago Copper		IA/11/84
1888	4800	George L. Miller	distilling exec.	George A. Garnsey	IA/12/88/pl.
1891	4801	Joseph H. Howard	lumber merchant	Patton & Fisher	E/8/21/91
1891	4805	J. H. Witbeck	lumber merchant		CP/3/25/91
1892	4808	Nathan Manasse		F. B. Townsend	E/1/30/92
b. 1890	4811				R
1890	4812	C. T. Morse	attorney		CP/6/7/90
b. 1890	4819				R
b. 1890	4820				R
b. 1890	4823				R
1890	4824	J. J. Lindman	trader, Board of Trade	F. R. Schock	IA/8/90
1890	4828	Kate B. Parish		Henry H. Sprague	IA/7/90
b. 1890	4829				R
1889	4830	William Craig	builder		D
1892	4833	Edward C. Hale	bakery exec.	De Witt T. Kennard	E/9/3/92
1895	4837	N. L. Barmore	mfr. undertakers' supplies		CP/8/6/95
b. 1890	4840	Charles Listman	flour merchant	Henry H. Sprague	R; IA/4/91/pl.
b. 1890	4846				R
b. 1890	4847	E. J. Edwards	stock car mfr.		R; D
1889	4850	B. A. Ulrich	real estate broker	William Craig	HPN/5/4/89
1889	4853	C. W. Kirk	wholesale clothier	William Craig	HPN/6/8/89
1889	4857	C. E. Woodruff	wholesale clothier		HPN/6/8/89
1898	4860	Norman Carroll	broker	Frederick Perkins	IA/4/98; CN/3/9/98
1905	4901	E. A. Graff	brewer	William Pruyn, Jr.	CN/10/21/05
1904	4908	R. L. Gifford	engineer	Mortimer Gapper	CP/6/6/04
1909	4920	F. E. White	packer	Horatio Wilson	CN/11/20/09
1906	4926	H. B. Leavitt	pres. Leavitt Lumber Co.	William Pruyn, Jr.	CN/5/26/06
1903	4928	Kirk Hawes	attorney	William Pruyn, Jr.	CN/12/5/03

Date	Address	Owner	Occupation	Architect/Builder	Source
1905	4932, 4936	William Morris	sash & door mfr.	Doerr & Doerr	CN/11/11/05
1901	4933, 4941	Kirk Hawes	attorney	W. Pruyn, Jr.	CN/11/23/01
1910	4940	Charles Antoine	merchant	N. Max Dunning	CN/12/17/10
1902	4948	D. Hawes		William Pruyn, Jr.	CN/12/6/02

Woodlawn Avenue

Date	Address	Owner	Occupation	Architect/Builder	Source
1887	4729	H. M. S. Montgomery	grain commission merchant		R; D
b. 1890	4733	Silas Moore	real estate broker		R; D
1908	4800	Robert McDougal	trader, Board of Trade	Horatio Wilson	WA/6/10/pl.; CN/10/17/08
1873	4812	Christopher B. Bouton	mfr. structural iron		D
1910	4815	Thomas E. Wilson	packer	Howard Van Doren Shaw	CN/7/16/10
1902	4825	Lester Frankenthal	physician	Richard Schmidt (Hugh Garden)	CN/6/7/02
1907	4830	James Douglas	pres. American Cereal Co.	Howard Van Doren Shaw	CN/6/22/07
1903	4833	George Birkhoff, Jr.	real estate broker	W. S. Banfield	CN/2/14/03
1904	4838	Daniel N. Eisendrath	physician	Henry L. Ottenheimer	CN/12/10/04
1906	4841	Frank K. Hoover	engineer	William Carbys Zimmerman	CN/5/19/06
1902	4847	William F. Burrows	pres., Libby, McNeill	Frost & Granger	CN/8/23/02
1908	4900	Albert H. Wolf	engineer, contractor	Horatio Wilson	CN/4/4/08
1902	4901	Charles H. Starkweather		Howard Van Doren Shaw	B/8/06/pl.; CN/5/24/02; IA/4/05/pl.
1906	4905	Fred A. Price	insurance exec.	Horatio Wilson	CN/4/28/06
1903	4915, 4919	William Morris	sash & door mfr.	Doerr & Doerr	CN/11/14/03
1903	4924	Morris Rosenwald	clothing mfr.	Howard Van Doren Shaw	CN/6/8/03
1907	4925	Benjamin H. Conkling	insurance exec.	Horatio Wilson	IA/5/08/pl.; CN/4/20/07

Date	Address	Owner	Occupation	Architect/Builder	Source
1905	4929	Charles Scribner	electrical engineer	Horatio Wilson	CN/3/18/05
1906	4930	Walden Shaw	pres. Walden W. Shaw Livery Co.	Marshall & Fox	CN/11/17/06
1904	4933	Bernard E. Sunny	gen. mgr. General Electric	George Beaumont	CN/5/21/04
1905	4937	H. J. Flood	mfr. brick machinery	Robert S. Smith	CN/7/1/05
1908	4940	Frank B. Stone	lumber merchant	William Carbys Zimmerman	CN/4/4/08
1907	4943, 4945	George Birkhoff, Jr.	real estate broker	Horatio Wilson	CN/5/11/07
1910	4949	Charles Antoine	merchant		CP/11/26/10
b. 1890	4950 (moved from Greenwood)				R

Greenwood Avenue

Date	Address	Owner	Occupation	Architect/Builder	Source
1906*	4715–21	Charles Hallgren	painter	Andrew Sandegren	CN/10/13/06
1894	4729	J. W. Janney	general agent	Alfred Smith	CP/5/17/94
1904	4730	M. J. Moorehouse		J. B. Cole	CP/4/14/04
1897	4807	J. J. Dau	merchant	George Maher	B/9/03/pl.; IA/9/97
1904	4819	Joseph Schaffner	clothier	Holabird & Roche	CN/8/13/04
b. 1890	4826				R
1883	4830	J. A. Lane		Dixon & Townsend	T/10/14/83
1902	4840	Charles A. Goodyear	lumber merchant	William Carbys Zimmerman	CN/5/17/02
1895	4841	Richard Nash	packer	Pridmore & Stanhope	E/6/1/95; IA/6/95
1896	4857	John B. Lord	pres., Ayer, Lord Tie	Charles Frost	CP/6/15/96
1907	4900	Henry Veeder	attorney	Howard Van Doren Shaw	CN/8/10/07
1910	4906	Lois Cook Johnson		William Carbys Zimmerman	CN/5/21/10
1906	4907	Louis A. Kohn	wholesale clothier	Alfred A. Alschuler	IA/12/07/pl.; CN/3/10/06

Date	Address	Owner	Occupation	Architect/Builder	Source
1896	4911	Cornelia McLaury		Howard Van Doren Shaw	IA/7/97/pl.; E/7/25/96
1898	4914	Robert Vierling	iron & steel mfr.	H. H. Waterman & Dwight H. Perkins	CN/12/7/98
1896	4917	Charles E. Gill	exec., Chicago Law Publishers	W. A. Otis	IA/9/89/pl.; E/7/18/96
1901	4920	Enos M. Barton	pres. Western Electric	Frost & Granger	AR/10/01/pl.
1896	4923	L. A. Carton	packer	W. A. Otis	E/7/25/96
1890	4928	P. Becher			CP/10/3/90
1907	4930	Ernest J. Magerstadt	city collector	George Maher	CN/4/27/07
1888	4935	Edward Turner	dry goods merchant	Solon S. Beman	BB/5/31/88
1899	4935 (barn)	Adolphus W. Green	attorney	Daniel Burnham	CN/5/3/99
b. 1886	4950	John C. Welling	vice-pres. ICRR		IA/5/86
b. 1886	5000	J. N. Barker			T/3/25/86
c. 1899	5001	D. F. Bremner	pres., National Biscuit Co.		D
1899	5009	D. F. Bremner	pres., National Biscuit Co.	Wilson & Marshall	CN/5/31/99
b. 1890	5016	C. H. Hawkins	agt. iron mfrs.		D
1905	5017	Homer H. Stillwell	merchant	Jarvis Hunt	CN/2/25/05; IA/11/06/pl.
1892	5022	George A. Tripp	stamped-metal mfr.	Treat & Foltz	E/6/14/92
1892	5026	William O. Goodman	lumber merchant	Treat & Foltz	T/2/14/92
1906	5040	A. R. Clarke	contractor	A. R. Clarke	CP/1/31/06
1910	5046	A. R. Clarke	contractor	Bishop & Co.	CN/5/28/10

Ellis Avenue

Date	Address	Owner	Occupation	Architect/Builder	Source
1893	4739	D. N. Hanson	woolens merchant	William Thomas	CP/11/25/93
1899	4745	William T. Fenton	banker	Wilson & Marshall	CN/4/12/99
1892	4800	Edward C. Potter	engineer, chemist	Charles Frost	CP/3/24/92; IA/4/96/pl.
1908	4801	J. C. Hutchins	attorney	Horatio Wilson	WA/2/10/pl.

Date	Address	Owner	Occupation	Architect/Builder	Source
1894	4810	J. C. Hutchins	attorney	Charles Frost	E/3/24/94
1908	4815	Harry D. Oppenheimer	packer	Horatio Wilson	CN/6/13/08
1896	4821	C. H. Canby		A. M. F. Colton	E/9/26/96
1891	4822	A. C. Buttolph	wholesale grocer		CP/3/25/91
1890	4832	Alonzo N. Fuller	wholesale grocer	Frederick Perkins	IA/2/90
1891	4840	Frank Fuller	wholesale grocer	Frederick Perkins	IA/1/92; T/1/11/91
1902	4845	Elliott H. Phelps		Wilson & Marshall	IA/2/02
1897	4848	Gustavus F. Swift	packer	Flanders & Zimmerman	CN/10/20/97
1897	4849	S. A. Spry	lumber merchant	Huel & Schmidt	IA/12/97
1899	4900	Benjamin Marshall	architect	Wilson & Marshall	CN/6/7/99; IA/3/02/pl.
1903	4901	Julius Rosenwald	vice-pres. Sears, Roebuck	Nimmons & Fellows	IA/4/05/pl.; CN/1/31/03
1899	4906	Benjamin Marshall	architect	Wilson & Marshall	CN/6/7/99; IA/3/02/pl.
b. 1890	4908				R
1894	4914	A. F. Collins			CP/2/21/94
1905	4918, 4920	Sol Wedels	builder		CN/4/8/05
1907	4921	Julius Weil	wholesale clothier	Alfred Alschuler	RI
1890	4924	P. Becher			CP10/3/90
1899	4932	Horatio Wilson	architect	Wilson & Marshall	CN/5/5/99
1898	4936	Horatio Wilson	architect	Wilson & Marshall	CN/11/23/98
1891	4938, 4940, 4942, 4944	C. A. Marshall		Wilson & Marble	T/12/6/91
1896	4950	H. M. Wilcox	attorney	Wilson & Marshall	E/2/1/96
1904	4954	W. S. Reed		John E. Youngberg	CN/3/26/04
1908	5001	William M. Crilly	contractor	William Carbys Zimmerman	CN/5/30/08
1908	5009	David Yondorf	clothier	Alfred Alschuler	CN/8/1/08
1895	5016	J. Woodhead	manager	Diven & White	E/12/14/95
1908*	5020	A. Hoefield	clothier	Henry Newhouse	CN/4/18/08
1909*	5024	E. Schoenfeld	attorney	George Maher	CN/10/9/09

Date	Address	Owner	Occupation	Architect/Builder	Source
1909*	5028	Joseph De Lee	physician	George Maher	CN/10/9/09
1910	5028 (garage)	Charles De Lee	manager	Van Holst & Fyfe	CN/10/29/10
1910	5036	Henry C. Hart	merchant	Holabird & Roche	CN/8/6/10
1906	5039, 5045	A. R. Clarke & Co.	developers	Bishop & Co.	CN/2/3/06
1907	5046	A. R. Clarke	developers	A. R. Clarke	CP/4/17/07
1907	5051	A. R. Clarke	developers	A. R. Clarke	CP/6/7/07
1910	5052	Jacob Franks	broker	Henry Newhouse	CN/10/8/10

Drexel Boulevard

Date	Address	Owner	Occupation	Architect/Builder	Source
1901	4801	Moses Born	clothier	Frost & Granger	IA/4/03/pl.; CN/2/23/01
1910	4805	G. B. Robbins	pres. Armour Car lines	Horatio Wilson	CN/7/9/10
1887	4845	Martin A. Ryerson		Treat & Foltz	T/1/9/87
1901	4935 (coach house only)	Simon Mandel	merchant	Frost & Granger	IA/4/03/pl.; CN/9/28/01
1890	4938	John A. McGill	physician	Henry Ives Cobb	IA/1/92; IA/8/96; CP/7/8/90
1887	4941	John H. Nolan	insurance exec.	Burnham & Root	BB/6/30/87
1903*	823 Drexel Square	A. S. Jackson		Myron Hunt	CN/2/14/03

East 48th Street

Date	Address	Owner	Occupation	Architect/Builder	Source
1901	1000	William T. Fenton	banker	Wilson & Marshall	T/9/15/01; IA/7/02/pl.; IA/8/04/pl.
1888	1019	D. O. Strong	real estate broker	Solon S. Beman	BB/5/31/88
1889	1020	Eldredge M. Fowler	manufacturer, reapers		HPN/6/8/89
b. 1890	1025				R
1897	1120	James J. Wait	"manager"	Dwight Perkins	B/11/03/pl.; IA/1/98; CN/6/16/97
b. 1887	1125	S. M. Moore	real estate broker		D

Date	Address	Owner	Occupation	Architect/Builder	Source
b. 1890	1126				R
1892	1130, 1136	Thomas Foster			CP/5/10/92
1886	1300	William R. Page	attorney	Jenney & Otis	HPN/12/4/86; BB/11/86
1905*	1340–48	William Reed		John Youngberg	CN/10/7/05
1901*	1352–54	Frank Gustafson	real estate developer	Andrew Sandegren	CN/4/27/01
1907*	1358–64			Andrew Sandegren	CN/9/28/07
1867	1357–59	Jonathan Kennicott	dentist		CR
1908*	1365–67	Charles W. Hoff	real estate developer	Charles W. Hoff	CP/4/23/08

East 49th Street

Date	Address	Owner	Occupation	Architect/Builder	Source
b. 1890	933, 935				R
1892	1030	Solon S. Beman	architect		D
1890	1031, 1033, 1035, 1037, 1039	Walter Johnson	physician		CP/10/90
1907	1332	George Blossom	insurance exec.	Frank Lloyd Wright	
1894	1346, 1350, 1354, 1360	Clara Turner			CP/10/13/94

East 50th Street

Date	Address	Owner	Occupation	Architect/Builder	Source
1901	924	Albert H. Loeb	sec. Sears, Roebuck	Henry Newhouse	CN/1/12/01
1867	1030	Ezra Brainerd	real estate developer		RI
b. 1890	1031				R
1905	1219	L. D. Kellogg	attorney	W. A. Otis	CN/7/15/05
1905	1223, 1225	A. C. Barnes; C. E. Murison		J. E. O. Pridmore	CN/5/20/05
b. 1890	1229	John Dunham	sugar merchant		R
b. 1890	1243	John Dunham	sugar merchant		R
1886	1309	A. W. Green	"agent"		HPH/3/13/86
1901	1315–17–19	J. D. Hawes	real estate developer	George Williams	CP/11/27/01

138

Date	Address	Owner	Occupation	Architect/Builder	Source
1901	1323–27–31	J. D. Hawes	real estate developer	W. H. Pruyn, Jr.	CN/10/7/01
1900*	1361–63	J. D. Hawes	real estate developer	George Williams	CP/11/14/00
1904*	1411–13			G. Allen	CP/4/28/04

Madison Park

Date	Address	Owner	Occupation	Architect/Builder	Source
1902	1310	Kirk Hawes	attorney	W. H. Pruyn, Jr.	CN/6/7/02
1897	1316	Kirk Hawes	attorney	W. H. Pruyn, Jr.	CN/11/24/97

Notes

NOTES TO CHAPTER 1

1. A. T. Andreas, *History of Chicago* (Chicago: A. T. Andreas, 1884) 2:479.

2. Ibid., 1:129.

3. Local title searches.

4. A. T. Andreas, *History of Cook County* (Chicago: A. T. Andreas, 1884), p. 536.

5. Personal communication, Paul Adrien Cornell.

6. Andreas, *Cook County,* p. 528.

7. Andreas, *Chicago,* 2:449.

8. Andreas, *Cook County,* pp. 542–43.

9. *Chicago Press and Tribune,* Apr. 13, 1859.

10. Andreas, *Cook County,* p. 555.

11. Ibid., p. 513.

12. Ibid., p. 531.

13. Bessie Louise Pierce, *A History of Chicago* (Chicago: Alfred A. Knopf, 1940), 2:327.

14. *Town of Hyde Park Annual Report* (Chicago: Rand McNally and Co., 1869).

15. Andreas, *Cook County,* p. 557.

16. Victoria Post Ranney, *Olmsted in Chicago* (Chicago: R. R. Donnelley and Sons, 1972), pp. 25–31.

17. Paul M. Angle, *The Great Chicago Fire* (Chicago: Chicago Historical Society, 1971), pp. 31–36.

18. John M. Van Osdel, "History of Chicago Architecture" (*Inland Architect* 1 (1883): 36–37.

19. Pierce, *Chicago,* 2:103–5.

20. *Inland Architect* 22 (1893): 28.

NOTES TO CHAPTER 2

1. Andreas, *Cook County,* p. 215.

2. *Chicago Tribune,* Dec. 4, 1879.

3. Ibid., Dec. 5, 1879.

4. *Hyde Park Annual Report,* 1880.

5. Ibid., 1882.

6. *Chicago Herald,* Nov. 3, 1887.

7. Charles Root, "Memories of Hyde Park," unpub. ms, Chicago Historical Society.

8. *Chicago Tribune,* June 2, 1878.

9. Ibid., Mar. 25, 1887.

10. J. D. Hibbard, "Hyde Park Fire Department," unpub. ms, Chicago Historical Society.

11. *Annual Reports of the Village of Hyde Park.*

12. *Hyde Park Herald,* Aug. 26, 1886.

13. *Memorial Volume: An Account of the Tri-Cennial Class Meeting of 1854, Union College* (Hyde Park, Illinois: Hyde Park Publishing Co., 1884) pp. 41–42.

14. *Chicago Tribune,* July 15, 1872.

15. Ibid., Dec. 14, 1873.

16. Ibid., Jan. 30, 1876.

17. Ibid., Feb. 6, 1876.

18. Stanley Buder, *Pullman: An Experiment in Industrial Order and Community Planning, 1880–1930* (New York, Oxford University Press, 1967), p. 110.

19. *Chicago Tribune,* Apr. 8, 1877.

20. Ibid., May 11, 12, 19, Sept. 1, 1878.

21. Ibid., Mar. 16, 22, 1879; Feb. 18, 1882; Feb. 7, 11, Mar. 11, 15, Apr. 4, 8, 1883; Mar. 25, 1884; Mar. 28, 1885; Mar. 21, 28, Apr. 3, 10, 1886.

22. Ibid., Mar. 16, 1879; Mar. 15, 29, 30, 1882; Mar. 12, 16, 25, 26, 1884; Mar. 15, 17, 19, 26, 1885; Mar. 12, 24, Apr. 9, 1886.

23. Ibid., Apr. 8, 1887; Mar. 23, 1879; Mar. 22, 30, 1882; Mar. 11, Apr. 8, 1883; Mar. 16, 19, 20, 22, 25, 28, 1884; Mar. 19, 21, 1885; Mar. 7, 21, 28, Apr. 7, 1886; *Hyde Park Herald,* Apr. 3, 10, 1886, Apr. 4, 1888.

24. *Chicago Tribune,* Jan. 19, 26, 1883; Mar. 1, 1885; *Hyde Park Herald,* Jan. 10, 1885.

25. *Hyde Park Annual Report,* 1882, 1884; *Chicago Tribune,* Jan. 19, 26, 1883; Mar. 1, 4, 15, 29, Apr. 2, 1885; *Hyde Park Herald,* Jan. 10, Feb. 7, 1885; May 1, 1886.

26. *Chicago Tribune,* Jan. 23, 30, Feb. 27, Sept. 18, Nov. 7, Nov. 13, 1887; *Chicago Herald,* Nov. 6, 1887; *Chicago Daily News,* Nov. 9, 1887.

27. *Hyde Park Herald,* Nov. 9, 1887; *Chicago Tribune,* Nov. 17, 1887; Jan. 8, 1888; *Chicago Herald,* Nov. 10, 1887; Mar. 16, 1888; *Proceedings of the Board of Trustees, Village of Hyde Park* (1887), p. 144; Pierce, *Chicago* (vol. 3, 1957), p. 332. See also Village of Hyde Park *v.* City of Chicago, Springfield, 124 Ill. 156 (Ill. S. Ct. 1888), John Dolese et al. *v.* Daniel A. Pierce, Springfield, 124 Ill. 140 (Ill. S. Ct. 1888).

28. *Chicago Herald,* Mar. 16, 1888.

29. Ibid., Jan. 13, 1889; *Chicago Tribune,* Jan. 13, 1889.

30. *Chicago Herald,* Jan. 16, 1889; *Chicago Tribune,* Jan. 20, Feb. 17, 1889.

31. *Chicago Herald,* Mar. 31, 1889.

32. *Chicago Daily News,* July 2, 1889.

33. *Chicago Tribune,* July 14, 1889.

34. Ibid., May 15, 1892.

35. Laura Willard, "The History of Hyde Park: A Study in Local Government" (1896), unpub. typescript, Chicago Historical Society.

36. *Chicago Tribune,* Nov. 9, 1879.

37. Ibid., May 16, 1880.

38. Letter from Charles Root to Alice Manning Dickey in *Hyde Park Herald Centennial Issue,* 1956.

39. *Chicago Tribune,* Sept. 8, 22, Nov. 13, 1881.

40. "The Mendelssohn Club of Hyde Park, 1877–1884," unpub. ms, Chicago Historical Society; *Tribune,* Sept. 29, 1881.

41. *Hyde Park Herald,* Jan. 19, 1884.

42. Ibid., Jan. 12, 26, Mar. 1, Oct. 4, 1884; Mar. 14, 1886; *Chicago Tribune,* Jan. 6, Feb. 3, 1889.

43. *Hyde Park Herald,* Apr. 17, 1886, June 3, 1887; Sept. 23, 1888.

44. Pierce, *Chicago,* 3:481.

45. *Chicago Tribune,* Nov. 13, 1881; May 6, 1888.

46. Pierce, *Chicago,* 3:477.

47. Andreas, *Cook County,* p. 561.

48. Muriel Beadle and the Centennial History Committee, *The Fortnightly of Chicago: The City and its Women, 1873–1973* (Chicago: Henry Regnery, 1973), pp. 9–11.

49. Henrietta Greenebaum Frank and Amalie Hofer Jerome (compilers), *Annals of the Chicago Woman's Club for the First Forty Years of Its Organization, 1876–1916* (Chicago: Chicago Woman's Club, 1916).

50. Andreas, *Chicago,* 3:424.

51. *Chicago Tribune,* Jan. 12, 1883; Jan. 18, Feb. 22, Mar. 2, 1884; *Hyde Park Herald,* Jan. 24, 1885.

52. Edward T. James (ed.), *Notable American Women, 1607–1950* (Cambridge: Harvard University Press, Belknap Press, 1971).

53. *Chicago Tribune,* Jan. 13, 1872.

54. James, *Notable American Women.* See also Catharine V. Waite scrapbook, Chicago Historical Society.

55. *University of Chicago Weekly,* Mar. 6, 1893, p. 10.

56. W. W. Boyington, "Architecture at the Present Time As Compared with That of Fifty Years Ago," *Inland Architect* 10 (1887): 51.

57. *Chicago Architect and Building News* 1 (1876): 111.

58. E. H. Taylor, "Domestic Architecture," *Inland Architect* 8 (1886): 22.

59. Russell Sturgis, John W. Root, Bruce Price, Donald G. Mitchell, Samuel Parsons, Jr., W. A. Linn, *Homes in City and Country* (New York: Charles Scribner's Sons, 1893), pp. 43–44.

60. Ibid., p. 63.

61. Francis Le Baron, "Mantels and Grates," *Inland Architect* 3 (1884): 48.

62. I. K. Pond, "The Home," *Inland Architect* 10 (1887): 63.

63. George W. Maher, "Originality in American Architecture," *Inland Architect* 10 (1887): 34.

64. George M. Barbour (ed.), *Sketch Book of the Exposition* (Chicago: Lakeside Press, 1883).

65. *Hyde Park Herald,* Feb. 19, 1884.

66. *Chicago Tribune,* May 13, 1883.

67. Francis Le Baron, "Stained Glass," *Inland Architect* 3 (1884): 76–7.

68. *Chicago Tribune,* Sept. 2, 1883.

69. *Chicago Tribune,* May 4, 1884.

70. *Inland Architect* 1 (1882): 2.

71. *Chicago Tribune,* Nov. 30, 1879; Dec. 9, 1883; Oct. 21, 1889; *Inland Architect* 4 (1884): 12.

72. *National Builder* 1 (1885): *The National Builder's Album of Beautiful Homes* (Chicago: National Builder's Publishing Co., 1891).

73. *Chicago Tribune,* Mar. 18, Apr. 19, 1874.

74. Ibid., Mar. 31, 1889.

75. Ibid., Aug. 25, 1872; Mar. 12, 1876; Feb. 24, Mar. 24, 1878; Mar. 28, 1880.

76. *Chicago Tribune,* Jan. 15, 1884.

77. Ibid., Dec. 23, 1883; Jan. 18, 1884; *Hyde Park Herald,* May 16, 1884; Feb. 14, May 16, 1885; *Inland Architect,* 3 (1884): 51.

78. *Chicago Tribune,* July 16, 1889.

NOTES TO CHAPTER 3

1. See Rossiter Johnson, *A History of the World's Columbian Exposition Held in Chicago in 1893* (New York: D. Appleton and Co., 1897).

2. *Chicago Tribune,* May 8, 1892.

3. *The Economist,* Sept. 17, 1892.

4. *Chicago Tribune,* Oct. 16, 1892.

5. Clara Louise Root Burnham, *Sweet Clover: A Romance of the White City* (New York: Grosset and Dunlap, 1893), p. 32.

6. Ibid., p. 69.

7. Lucretia Harper, "Hyde Park," unpub. typescript, Chicago Historical Society.

8. Frederick Law Olmsted, "The Landscape Architecture of the World's Columbian Exposition," *Inland Architect* 22 (1893): 19.

9. *Martin's World's Fair Album, Atlas and Family Souvenir: The Artistic Guide to Chicago and the World's Columbian Exposition* (Chicago: Columbian Art Co., 1893).

10. Burnham, *Sweet Clover,* pp. 153–54.

11. *University of Chicago Weekly,* Nov. 1893.

12. Ibid., Jan. 11, 1894.

13. *The Economist,* Jan. 11, 1893.

14. *Chicago Tribune,* Aug. 11, 1901.

15. Maud Howe Elliott (ed.), *Art and Handicraft in the Woman's Building of the World's Columbian Exposition* (Chicago and New York: Rand McNally, 1894), p. 21.

16. Ibid., p. 23.

17. *Chicago Tribune,* April 12, 1891.

18. George M. R. Twose, "Brickwork and Faience at the Fair," *Brickbuilder* 2 (1893): 64–6.

19. Perry R. Duis, "The Saloon and the Public City: Chicago and Boston, 1890–1920," vol. 1, (Ph.D. diss., University of Chicago, 1975) pp. 852–55.

20. Johnson, *History,* 1:359 ff.

21. Minutes and records of the Hyde Park Protective Association, Chicago Historical Society.

22. Thomas Wakefield Goodspeed, *A History of the University of Chicago* (Chicago: University of Chicago Press, 1916. Reprinted 1972, p. 6.

23. Papers of John D. Rockefeller, University of Chicago Library, box 1.

24. Papers of the American Baptist Education Society, University of Chicago Library, box 1, folder 1.

25. Rockefeller Papers.

26. Frederick Gates, "The Need of a Baptist University in Chicago," Rockefeller Papers, box 1, folder 3.

27. Frederick Gates to H. L. Morehouse, Oct. 23, 1888, Rockefeller Papers, box 1, folder 3.

28. George Northrup to William Rainey Harper, Dec. 6, 1888, Rockefeller Papers, box 1, folder 4.

29. Goodspeed, *History,* pp. 92–96.

30. Ibid., pp. 83 ff.

31. *Chicago Tribune,* Aug. 18, 1879.

32. Gates to Morehouse, Jan. 17, 1890, Rockefeller Papers, box 1, folder 9.

33. Robert Morss Lovett, *All Our Years* (New York: Viking Press, 1948), p. 54.

34. Douglas Sutherland, *Fifty Years on the Civic Front* (Chicago: Civic Federation, 1943).

35. "Introductory Biography," Papers of Charles E. Merriam, University of Chicago Library.

36. Ibid.

37. Sutherland, *Fifty Years,* p. 38.

38. Frank and Jerome, *Annals of Chicago Woman's Club.*

39. Lloyd Lewis and Henry Justin Smith, *Chicago: The History of its Reputation* (New York: Blue Ribbon Books, 1929), pp. 220–24.

40. Harper, "Hyde Park."

41. *Chicago Tribune,* Sept. 7, 8, 1901.

42. Ibid., Sept. 9, 1901.

43. Jane Addams, *Twenty Years at Hull House* (New York: Macmillan Co., 1945), p. 408.

44. William Vaughn Moody, *Poems and Poetic Dramas* (Boston: Houghton Mifflin Company, 1912), 1:55 ff.

45. Olivia Howard Dunbar, *A House in Chicago* (Chicago: University of Chicago Press, 1947).

46. Joseph Twyman, "The Art and Influence of William Morris," *Inland Architect* 42 (1904): 43–5.

47. Sharon S. Darling, *Chicago Metalsmiths* (Chicago: Chicago Historical Society, 1977), p. 39.

48. *The Arts and Crafts Movement in America, 1876–1916,* exhibit catalog (Princeton University, 1973).

49. *Chicago Tribune,* Jan. 13, 1901.

50. *House Beautiful,* Nov., 1906.

51. *The Economist,* Dec. 2, 1893.

52. *Chicago Tribune,* Jan. 12, 1901.

53. *Brickbuilder* 7 (1898): 1.

54. *University of Chicago Weekly,* Mar. 15, 1894.

55. *Chicago Tribune,* Mar. 30, 1902. See also archives of the South East Chicago Commission.

56. Minutes of Hyde Park Protective Association, July 14, 1909.

57. Homer N. Hoyt, *One Hundred Years of Land Values in Chicago, 1830–1933* (Chicago: University of Chicago Press, 1933), p. 189.

58. Pierce, *Chicago,* 3:208; *Chicago Tribune,* Jan. 26, Oct. 5, 1890, Sept. 22, Mar. 3, 1901.

59. *Chicago Tribune,* Apr. 21, 1901.

60. See *Construction News,* June 7, 22, Mar. 16, 1907, Nov. 19, 1908.

61. "Household Art and the Microbe," *House Beautiful,* Oct. 1899; *Chicago Tribune,* June 15, 1902; *House Beautiful,* June 1905.

62. Charles Richmond Henderson, *The Social Spirit in America* (Chicago: Scott, Foresman and Co., 1903), p. 37.

63. Charles Eugene Banks, *Beautiful Homes and Social Customs of America* (Chicago: Bible House, 1902), p. 27.

64. *The Economist,* Apr. 8, 1893.

65. *Chicago Tribune,* Aug. 11, 1901.

66. *Inland Architect* 27 (1896): 5.

67. Pierce, *Chicago,* 2:98–99; 3:112. See also Helen Swift, *My Father and My Mother* (Chicago: privately printed, 1937).

145

68. See Leonard Eaton, *Two Chicago Architects and Their Clients: Frank Lloyd Wright and Howard Van Doren Shaw* (Cambridge, Mass.: MIT Press, 1972).

69. Frank Lloyd Wright, *An Autobiography* (New York and London: Longmans, Green and Co., 1932), p. 78.

70. *The Economist,* May 21, June 18, 1892.

71. *House Beautiful,* June 1899, p. 40.

72. Personal communication, Mrs. Edgar B. Stern.

73. *United States Census,* 1900.

74. Goodspeed, *History,* pp. 169–70.

75. *Chicago Tribune,* Sept. 27, 1903.

76. Ibid., Jan. 18, 1903.

77. U. S. Census, 1900.

78. See H. Allen Brooks, *The Prairie School* (Toronto: University of Toronto Press, 1972).

79. *Inland Architect,* 45 (1905): 5.

80. Papers of Robert Herrick, University of Chicago Library, box 3, folder 10.

81. *Brickbuilder,* Sept. 1903.

NOTES FOR NOTES ON THE ARCHITECTS

1. *Construction News,* May 26, 1906, p. 401.

2. Ibid., Nov. 17, 1906.

3. Andreas, *History,* 3:72; *Construction News,* Oct. 22, 1904, p. 291.

4. Henry F. Withey and Elise Rathburn Withey, *Biographical Dictionary of American Architects (Deceased)* (Los Angeles: New Age Publishing Co., 1956).

5. *Industrial Chicago* (Chicago: Goodspeed Publishing Co., 1891).

6. *Illinois Society of Architects Monthly Bulletin,* Feb.–Mar. 1937.

7. Andreas, *History,* 3:451.

8. Goodspeed, *History,* p. 219.

9. Paul Gilbert and Charles Lee Bryson, *Chicago and Its Makers* (Chicago: Felix Mendelsohn, 1929), p. 967.

10. *Construction News,* June 16, 1906, p. 461.

11. Ibid., Oct. 14, 1905, p. 287.

12. Carl Condit, *The Chicago School of Architecture* (Chicago: University of Chicago Press, 1964), p. 59; see also Andreas, *History,* 3:74.

13. John W. Leonard, ed., *The Book of Chicagoans* (Chicago: A. N. Marquis, 1905).

14. *Construction News,* March 23, 1906, p. 323 (Garden); Dec. 10, 1904, p. 417 (Schmidt); see also Brooks, *Prairie School,* Condit, *Chicago School.*

146

15. Condit, *Chicago School,* pp. 116–17.

16. Personal communication, Mrs. Jon Peter Holsman.

17. *Construction News,* March 16, 1907, p. 191.

18. Ibid., Oct. 20, 1906, p. 323; see also J. William Rudd, "George W. Maher, Architect" (M.A. thesis, Northwestern University, 1964); Brooks, *Prairie School.*

19. *Construction News,* Oct. 24, 1903.

20. Leonard, *Chicagoans* (1917).

21. Gilbert and Bryson, *Chicago and Its Makers,* p. 871 (Marshall); *Construction News,* July 14, 1906, p. 23, (Fox).

22. *Who's Who in Chicago,* 1926.

23. *Construction News,* April 16, 1904, p. 207 (Nimmons); April 23, 1904 (Fellows); see also Brooks, *Prairie School* and Condit, *Chicago School.*

24. Condit, *Chicago School.*

25. *Construction News,* Nov. 3, 1906, p. 363.

26. *Construction News,* Nov. 9, 1907, p. 317; see also Brooks, *Prairie School,* and Condit, *Chicago School.*

27. Withey, *Biographical Dictionary.*

28. *Construction News,* Jan. 8, 1910, p. 70; Jan. 29, 1910; p. 18; see also Brooks, *Prairie School,* and Condit, *Chicago School.*

29. See David Lowe, *Lost Chicago* (Boston: Houghton Mifflin, 1975).

30. Eaton, *Two Chicago Architects;* Brooks, *Prairie School.*

31. Brooks, *Prairie School;* Condit, *Chicago School.*

32. Brooks, *Prairie School;* Condit, *Chicago School.*

33. Withey, *Biographical Dictionary.*

34. *Construction News,* May 12, 1906, p. 361.

35. Brooks, *Prairie School;* Condit, *Chicago School.*

Bibliography

HISTORICAL DEVELOPMENT

Histories

A. T. Andreas's *History of Chicago* (Chicago, 1884), in three volumes, and his *History of Cook County* are indispensable for information on the early days, as is Bessie Louise Pierce's *A History of Chicago* vols. 2, 3 (New York: A. A. Knopf, 1940, 1957; reprint, University of Chicago Press, 1975). The bibliography is extensive. Lucretia Harper's "Hyde Park," prepared for the Illinois Writers' Project in 1938–39 (in typescript at the Chicago Historical Society) contains some interesting information, but except for what is recognizable as coming from Andreas it is impossible to verify what she has to say. She has written in the margin: "I have not overlooked the bibliography. I had the sources written up, but some one in the library by mistake took them for scratch pads." Harold M. Mayer and Richard C. Wade's *Chicago: Growth of a Metropolis* (Chicago: University of Chicago Press, 1969) has passages and pictures relating to the neighborhood. Lloyd Lewis and Henry Justin Smith's *Chicago: The History of Its Reputation* (New York: Harcourt Brace, 1929) is lively and informative. The first chapter of Laura Willard's "History of Hyde Park" (typescript, 1895) is at the Historical Society. For the Columbian Exposition material, see Rossiter Johnson, ed., *A History of the World's Columbian Exposition Held in Chicago in 1893* (New York: Appleton, 1897) and H. N. Higgenbotham, *Report of the President to the Board of Directors of the World's Columbian Exposition* (Chicago: Rand McNally, 1898). Homer N. Hoyt in *One Hundred Years of Land Values in Chicago, 1830–1933* (Chicago: University of Chicago Press, 1933) illuminates the development of Chicago and its neighborhoods. *Pullman: An Experiment in Industrial Order and Community Planning, 1880–1930* (New York: Oxford University Press, 1967), by Stanley Buder, contains pertinent information.

Institutional Histories and Records

Thomas Wakefield Goodspeed's *A History of the University of Chicago: The First Quarter Century* (Chicago: University of Chicago Press, 1916) and his *History of the Hyde Park Baptist Church, 1874–1924* (published by the church) are both helpful, as is the *Fiftieth Anniversary Celebration—Hyde Park Presbyterian Church* (1910). *Fifty Years on the Civic Front,* by Douglas Sutherland (Chicago: The Civic Federation, 1943), *Annals of the Chicago Woman's Club for the First Fifty Years of Its Organization, 1866–1916* (Chicago Woman's Club, 1916), and *The Fortnightly of Chicago,* by Muriel Beadle and the Centennial Committee (Chicago: Henry Regnery, 1973), supply biographical material as well as the histories of these organizations. The Chicago Historical Society has the annual reports of the president and village officers of the village of Hyde Park for the fiscal years ending April 1, 1869–70, 1875, 1880, 1883–85, 1887–89. The minutes of the Hyde Park Protective Association and some of the records of the Hyde Park Fire Department are also at the Historical Society.

Biographical Sketches

Biographical material can be found in Andreas's *History of Chicago* and his *History of Cook County;* in *Chicago and its Makers,* by Paul Gilbert and Charles Lee Bryson (Chicago: Felix Mendelsohn, 1929); *Notable American Women, 1607–1950,* edited by Edward T. James (Cambridge, Mass.: Belknap Press of Harvard University, 1971); Thomas Wakefield Goodspeed, *The University of Chicago Biographical Sketches* (Chicago: University of Chicago Press, 1925); and *The Book of Chicagoans* (Chicago: A. N. Marquis, 1905).

Memoirs, Letters, Biographies, and Autobiographies

Edgar Goodspeed's *As I Remember* (New York: Harper and Bros., 1953); *All Our Years: The Autobiography of Robert Morss Lovett* (New York: Viking Press, 1948); and Francis W. Shepardson, "An Historical Sketch," in *The University of Chicago President's Report,* July 1897–July 1898, contain material on the early days of the University of Chicago, as do Robert Herrick's papers (University of Chicago Library, Department of Special Collections, box 6, folders 4, 8). Discussions of reasons for choosing Chicago as the site of the new University of Chicago can be found in the papers of the American Baptist Education Society (Special Collections, box 1, folder 1) and in the papers of John D. Rockefeller, Founder (box 1, folders 1–9), where they are arranged by date. Notes of reminiscences by Charles P. Root and Hamilton B. Bogue are in the manuscript room of the Chicago Historical Society. Janet Ayer recalls "Old Hyde Park" in Caroline Kirkland's *Chicago Yesterdays* (1919). "Utopia by the Railroad Tracks," a sketch of Rosalie Court, by Emmet Bay, for the Chicago Literary Club (May 2, 1949), is in the Newberry Library. *The Great Chicago Fire,* with an introduction and notes by Paul M. Angle (Chicago Historical Society, 1971), contains descriptions of the fire by individuals who experienced it. *My Father and My Mother,* by Helen Swift (privately printed, 1937), is a history of the Swift family. *Mary McDowell, Neighbor,* by Howard E. Wilson (Chicago: University of Chicago Press, 1928), and *Twenty Years at Hull House,* by Jane Addams (New York: Macmillan Co., 1945), deal with movements that affected the neighborhood in many ways.

Literature and Literary Criticism

The novels of Robert Herrick, particularly *The Web of Life* (New York: Macmillan Co., 1900), *Memoirs of an American Citizen* (New York: Macmillan Co., 1905), and *Chimes,* New York: Macmillan Co., 1926) offer a writer's portrait of Chicago. I. K. Friedman, *By Bread Alone* (New York: McClure, Phillips and Co., 1901), William Vaughn Moody, *Poems and Poetic Dramas* (Boston and New York: Houghton Mifflin, 1912), and Robert Morss Lovett, *Richard Gresham* (New York: Macmillan Co., 1904), are examples of local writing that confronts the problems of industrialization. Analysis of the literary movement in Chicago is dealt with in *The Rise of Chicago as a Literary Center from 1885 to 1920* by Hugh Duncan (Totowa, N.J.: Bedminster Press, 1964), *The Chicago Renaissance in American Letters,* by Bernard Duffey (Lansing: Michigan State University Press, 1954), and *Chicago Renaissance: The Literary Life in the Midwest: 1900–1930* (New York: Appleton-Century, 1966), by Dale Kramer. *A House in Chicago,* by Olivia Howard Dunbar (Chicago: University of Chicago Press, 1947), contains material on William Vaughn Moody and other poets of his time. Clara Louise Burnham Root's novel, *Sweet Clover: A Romance of the White City* (New York: Grosset and Dunlap, 1894), is as interesting for the social attitudes it depicts as for its descriptions of the fair.

Guidebooks

Early guidebooks include Everett Chamberlin, *Chicago and its Suburbs* (Chicago: 1874), *Chicago: A Hand Book for Strangers and Tourists* (Chicago: Halpin, Hayes and McClurg, 1869), James Runnion, *Out of Town* (Chicago: Western News Co., 1869), *The Inter-State Exposition Souvenir* (Chicago: Van Arsdale Massie, 1879), *Sketch Book of the Exposition,* edited by George M. Barbour (Chicago: Lakeside Press, 1883), *Martin's World's Fair Album-Atlas and Family Souvenir: The Artistic Guide to Chicago and the World's Columbian Exposition* (Chicago: Columbian

Art Co., 1893), and Hubert Howe Bancroft, *The Book of the Fair* (Chicago: Bancroft Co., 1895).

Brochures

Picturesque Kenwood (Craig and Messervy, 188–[?]) and *A Holiday at Rosalie Villas* (James P. Craig, 1888) contain pictures of houses; the latter also shows some interiors. The Chicago Historical Society has both.

Newspapers

The city newspapers, particularly the *Chicago Tribune* and the *Chicago Daily News,* are fruitful sources for material both on the history of the community and the development of its housing. The Historical Society has a few issues of the *Hyde Park Herald* between 1887 and 1889 and the *Hyde Park News* for 1886 to 1889. The *University of Chicago Weekly* contains some neighborhood news; old copies are to be found in the library's Department of Special Collections.

Maps

The Historical Society has two sets of maps, both essential for the understanding of the growth of the neighborhood: *Van Vechten and Snyder's Real Estate Map of Cook and DuPage Counties* (Chicago, 1875) and *Rascher's Atlas of Hyde Park, 1890*. The latter shows every house standing in 1890, what it was made of, how many stories, and what kind of roof and basement it had. Not all the addresses are still correct, but it is a prodigious work and immensely helpful. Donnelley's *Atlas of Chicago, 1905* is useful for the later period. There is a copy in the map room of the Regenstein Library.

Directories

There are a number of directories for the early years: *Halpin and Bailey, Edward, Udall and Hopkins,* among others. These can be found at the Historical Society. *The Lakeside Directories,* which start in 1874, are indispensable for verifying addresses. The early ones also give the tenant's occupation. The 1909 *Lakeside Directory* gives the changes in addresses for the east-west streets. Smaller directories, such as the *Blue Book* (1890–1915), *Lakeside Directories of Hyde Park* (1883, 1887, 1888, 1889), the *Elite* (1880–90, 1898–99), and the address lists of the faculty of the University of Chicago are more easily scanned, but have the disadvantage of listing only limited groups of people. Membership lists of the Literary Club, the Caxton Club, the Cliff Dwellers, the Merchants Club, the Commercial Club, the Fortnightly, and the Chicago Woman's Club offer insights into the social and intellectual relationships among residents.

Population Records

The United States Census Reports for 1870, 1880, and 1900 contain much information otherwise unavailable.

Supplementary Background Material

Additional information filling out the picture of life in the community and in the home can be found in the following: Perry R. Duis, *The Saloon and the Public City: Chicago and Boston, 1890–1910, I* (University of Chicago Ph.D. Dissertation, 1975), Victoria Post Ranney, *Olmsted in Chicago* (Chicago: R. R. Donnelley and Sons, 1972), *Memorial Volume: An Account of the Tri-Cennial Class Meeting of the Class of 1854, Union College, Schenectady, New York* (Hyde Park, Ill.: Hyde Park Publishing Company, 1885), Sharon S. Darling, *Chicago Metalsmiths* (Chicago: Chicago Historical Society, 1977), *The Arts and Crafts Movement in America, 1876–1916* (Princeton University Exhibit Catalogue, Princeton, N.J., 1973), Dena J. Epstein, *Music Publishing in Chicago before 1871: The Firm of Root and Cady, 1858–1871* (Detroit, Mich.: Detroit Studies in Music Biography 14, Information Coordinators, 1969), Charles Richmond Henderson, *The Social Spirit in America* (Chicago: Scott, Foresman, 1903), Charles Eugene Banks, *Beautiful Homes and Social Customs of America* (Chicago: Bible House, 1902), David Lowe, *Lost Chicago* (Boston: Houghton Mifflin, 1975), *Art and Handicraft in the Woman's Building of the World's Columbian Exposition,* edited by Maud E. Elliott (Chicago: Rand McNally and Co., 1894), Will Ransom, *Private Presses and Their Books* (New York: Philip C. Duschnes, 1963).

THE HOUSES AND THEIR ARCHITECTURE

Public Records

For houses built after 1890, that is, after annexation, the original permit, if there was one, can be obtained at City Hall. If the house was built before 1890 the title has to be traced back in the tract books which are kept in the office of the County Recorder, in the County Building. The original Hyde Park–Kenwood permits have disappeared. The County Assessor's Office will provide an estimate of the age of a house, but it can be wrong by as much as thirty or forty years.

Private Records

Many residents still have in their possession the title searches going back to when the land was first purchased. Some also have the original plans for their houses. Although this study has not dealt with interiors at all, the house plans could be of great value for a more profound architectural analysis than has been made here.

Periodicals

Professional journals, trade papers, and women's magazines provide material on houses and home furnishings not to be found elsewhere. The Burnham Library of the Art Institute of Chicago has copies of the professional journals, *Inland Architect, Northwestern Architect, Architectural Record, Architectural Review,* and *Western Architect.* Trade papers in the Burnham Library include *Brickbuilder* and *Building Budget. Construction News* and *The National Builder* are available at the Center for Research Libraries, *The Economist* at the Chicago Historical Society. Particularly interesting for its picture of tastes in home furnishings and the changing role of women is *House Beautiful,* also in the Burnham Library.

Books on Architecture

A great deal has been written about Chicago architecture. The most useful of these books for this particular study have been *Industrial Chicago: The Building Interests* (Chicago: Goodspeed Publishing Co., 1891), *Old Chicago Houses,* by John Drury (Chicago: University of Chicago Press, 1941), *Architecture in Old Chicago,* by Thomas Eddy Tallmadge (Chicago: University of Chicago Press, 1941), *The Chicago School of Architecture,* by Carl Condit (Chicago: University of Chicago Press, 1964), and H. Allen Brooks, *The Prairie School* (Toronto: University of Toronto Press, 1972). Henry F. Withey and Elise Rathburn Withey, *Biographical Dictionary of American Architects (Deceased)* (Los Angeles: New Age Publishing Co., 1956), contains some useful information. Special studies of interest include the following: Thomas Tallmadge, "The Chicago School," *Architectural Record,* March 1905, pp. 201–7, Leonard Eaton, *Two Chicago Architects and Their Clients: Frank Lloyd Wright and Howard Van Doren Shaw* (Boston: MIT Press, 1969), Henry-Russell Hitchcock, *In the Nature of Materials: The Buildings of Frank Lloyd Wright, 1874–1941* (New York: Hawthorne Books, 1942), Frank Lloyd Wright, *An Autobiography* (New York: Longmans, Green, 1932), Thomas S. Hines, *Burnham of Chicago: Architect and Pioneer* (New York: Oxford University Press, 1974), Hugh Morrison, *Louis Sullivan* (New York: W. W. Norton, 1935), James D. Kornwolf, *M. H. Baillie Scott and the Arts and Crafts Movement*) Baltimore: Johns Hopkins Press, 1972), Russell Sturgis, John W. Root, Bruce Price, Donald G. Mitchell, Samuel Parsons, Jr., and W. A. Linn, *Homes in City and Country* (New York: Charles Scribner's Sons, 1893), Susan J. Friedman, "The Prairie School Row Houses at Woodlawn and 56th" (typescript, University of Chicago, Special Collections), and Albert Tannler, "The Creation of Charles Hitchcock Hall, 1900–1902," *University of Chicago Library Society Bulletin* (Fall, 1975). See also *The Prairie School Review* for special issues devoted to individual architects of the Prairie School.

Index